MASTERING
MANAGEMENT

MASTERING MANAGEMENT

12 Keys to Managing a Growing Business

Doug Alexander

To order additional copies of this book, contact:
Xlibris Corporation
1-888-795-4274
www.Xlibris.com
Orders@Xlibris.com
40148

CONTENTS

DEDICATION

This book is dedicated to my wife Nancy,
the wisest person I know.
I could not do what I do without
her encouragement and counsel.

ACKNOWLEDGEMENTS

The ideas put forth in this book would not have been possible without the "success or failure" system that defines and drives our efforts in the free-market, capitalist environment in which American businesses operate. All of our efforts in overcoming obstacles and maximizing opportunities yield consequences which can broadly be defined as success or failure for us as individuals and, more importantly, for our enterprise. While government regulations play an increasing role in our business strategies, the potential for success or failure based upon our competitive ability continues to exist. The rewards can be great and the failures can be disastrously complete.

Even before "transparency" became a business buzzword, transparency existed in our American business environment to an extent greater than in any other. One of the good things about transparency is that we can learn from each other. "Learn" in this context means to understand why something was done and modify it properly and apply it usefully to our own situation. Here's to the men and women who put it all on the line to make American business what it is today—and what it will become in the years ahead.

FOREWORD

Much has been written lately about several areas of concern to American business: the culture of the workplace, employee empowerment, customer expectations, customer satisfaction, corporate social responsibility, and leadership. Some writers and commentators have suggested that these issues have been thoroughly explored and that it is time to move "forward," as if there is no more than a tangential connection of these issues to enterprise and the dynamics that make change the only constant in today's business environment. Could there be more to say, or just different ways of saying the same things that have been said before? Are there no real differences in management style? Is it just a matter of perspective and priority?

I don't think so, and that's why the issues mentioned above are among those discussed in this book. The reason for their inclusion lies in two simple truths: these areas of business are constantly changing, evolving, reinventing themselves as companies mature, and these topics are as important today to any successful business venture as they have always been. Even if perspective and priority were the only differences in the discussion, they may make all the difference between success and failure in the application of values to your prevailing corporate culture.

If you don't believe that, just ignore those areas and see what happens.

As important as it is for businesses to integrate their various departments into a seamless, efficient operation, it is equally important for each discipline within an organization to function independent of another when circumstances so dictate. How well a business does this is dependent upon many things, the most important of which are the subjects of this book. The subject matter of each chapter is approached from a generalist perspective. Years of work in American business both large and small, under all types of economic conditions in both manufacturing and service-producing endeavors, have given me a unique perspective from which to draw insights and conclusions.

Anyone who loves the challenges and rewards of the business environment will appreciate this book. Whether your business is large or small, the examples will provide insight for newly minted managers, affirmation or caution signals regarding the actions contemplated during uncertain scenarios for any manager, and knowing nods from men and women of letters (e.g., CEO, COO, CFO). There are certainly pros and cons to working for either a large or small enterprise. For example, in a small company you can (indeed, you probably must) wear several hats, whereas those same actions in a large company could be considered interdepartmental intrusion. Most would agree that, for most individuals, it is harder to be "noticed" in a large company, but you will probably get a better benefits package than what would be available in a smaller firm. Larger companies are almost always, of necessity, more formal in their organizational and operational management styles. The list could go on and on, and occasionally the jump from a smaller to a larger organization (or vice versa) can be a challenging experience due to the differences in the prevailing corporate culture. This book would not have been possible had I not been privileged to spend considerable time in a position to share in the planning, emotions, successes, and failures of some of the tremendously talented and dedicated business people who make American business work.

Would we all work this hard, be this creative, or take these risks were it not for the reward potential of privately owned businesses, operating in a free-market capitalist society? Probably not. The potentials within risk/reward performance and the success/failure potential of a competitive business environment make it all worthwhile.

Each chapter in this book is prefaced by a quote from the late Vince Lombardi, head coach of the NFL's Green Bay Packers from 1959 to 1967. A man whose life is the subject of entire books, suffice it to say that he was a man with high ethical standards and consistent values who demanded the best from each of his players and who had an exceptional ability to determine whether that expectation was being met by each individual. He talked much about life and how it should be lived, and I find little with which to disagree. I hope you find his thoughts inspiring and thought provoking.

Throughout this book, the words *corporation* and *company* and *corporate* are used to mean not specifically these types of entities, but also proprietorships, partnerships, organizations, and other types of legal cooperatives under which business is conducted. I have, in this book, made every effort to eliminate business "jargon" and words such as *floccinaucinihilipilification* (look it up). My interest is neither to impress nor to confuse, but to express ideas in such a way as to enable you to come to that Eureka! conclusion that has so far eluded you, or to validate or invalidate your ideas about American enterprise and what makes it work.

INTRODUCTION

> "Winning is not a sometime thing: It's
> an all the time thing. You don't win
> once in a while; you don't do the right
> thing once in a while; you do them right
> all the time. Winning is a habit.
> Unfortunately, so is losing."
> —Vincent Lombardi

One of the great novels of the 20th century is Thornton Wilder's *The Bridge of San Luis Rey*. The curriculum in the Great Literature classes at the educational institutions that I surveyed would not include this work in their required readings as they did when I was a student. Nevertheless, it is a highly engaging story that provides the reader with many thought-provoking situations.

This Pulitzer Prize-winning book opens as citizens of a tiny town in Peru begin to deal with the aftermath of the collapse of a footbridge just outside the town, killing the five pedestrians who were crossing the bridge. As the book unfolds, we trace the lives of the five victims, strangers to each other, and what brought them all together at that particular time on that particular bridge. This information comes to us because of the efforts of Brother Juniper, a monk in the town, who witnessed the collapse and wondered why this group of five had been destined to come together and to die at such a time, in such a way.

As in the book, groups of five, five hundred, or even five thousand people come together every day all across the world. They do this to accomplish tasks that require group effort. We spend little or no time thinking about what brought these individuals together: their backgrounds, their motivations, their hopes, their dreams, their view of life. You are part of such a group. You spend as much time in your productive life as an interactive member of a work group as you do with your family or friends—maybe more.

During your working lifetime, it is likely that you will move from group to group. It is also likely that, within these groups, your status relative to other group members will change, for better or for worse. How you interact as an individual and how the group as a whole functions is vitally important to the individuals and to the group. Success and failure are real and not without consequence, both for the group and for those who populate it. Your participation as a co-worker in an American enterprise can and should inspire and empower you. No matter what your position, an impressive legacy can be left by working creatively, efficiently, and ethically throughout your productive life.

Your co-workers, who are fellow members of your group, come from all walks of life, and while their life experiences are probably not unique to the group, they may well be unique to the individual at that point in time. Does a co-worker have seemingly insurmountable financial worries? Did the co-worker argue with his or her spouse this morning? Is he or she dealing with serious family or personal health problems? Is he or she mourning the death of a family member, co-worker, or pet? Except in rare instances, you do not know, and to a great extent, you do not care. This is not to say that you should not offer what assistance you can, but not at the expense of the efficiency and the goals of your group.

You and your co-workers gather about 250 days each year to put the trials, tribulations, and happiness of the rest of life aside to focus on specific tasks and to accomplish specific goals. How successfully this happens is dictated to a large extent by the prevailing corporate culture of the company. It is as impossible to overstate the importance and the effect of corporate culture as it is to escape it. It exists everywhere people come together to accomplish tasks, and how you deal with it can literally define your role in corporate life in American business.

American business is a wonderful thing. Virtually everything that is produced, invented, serviced, and marketed today is done so through a structured business enterprise. This is true for the service and professional business sectors as well. We have created a tremendous free-enterprise corporate workforce and marketplace that meets people's needs for products and services on a global scale.

In most traditional households today, the husband and wife are both in the workforce, and it is not a given that the husband is the primary wage earner. Just 50 years ago, the stereotypical family image was that of a husband saying goodbye to his children and his stay-at-home wife for 40-plus hours a week as he left for the plant or the office. That is no longer the case. How amazing that in just five decades, American business has expanded to welcome the talents and abilities of millions of women. Rather than being simply "additional workers," women now play an indispensable role in all facets of corporate life. More on this later.

Another change is that more than half of us work for companies that did not exist 50 years ago or in jobs that did not exist then. Even many of those who work in old-line jobs that are still around today would find little resemblance between their jobs today and those of their predecessors 50 years ago. While the objective may be the same, the introduction of technology alone would render the primary tasks of 50 years ago virtually obsolete. The use of technologically innovative tools in the workplace, while difficult to quantify, has always held the promise of increased efficiency, fewer mistakes, and more accurate and timely information, and it has delivered on those promises. Any IT professional (talk about a job that didn't exist 50 years ago!) will tell you that we are just beginning to see the productive corporate benefits of technology.

Couple the productive benefits of technology with the addition of millions of women and now-aging baby boomers to the workforce, and the staggering job-creating capability over the last 50 years of American business becomes even more apparent, even to those still skeptical about our free-enterprise system. Compare our corporate history with that of any other country or continent, and the American free-enterprise advantage becomes quickly apparent.

Another reality introduced to American business over the last 50 years is the increased involvement of government in the overall operations as well as the day-to-day operational aspects of business enterprises. Government involvement manifests itself chiefly in the form of regulations, which are enacted, imposed and monitored by federal agencies. Few, if any, sectors of American business are unaffected by government oversight, some certainly to a greater degree than others. Government agencies such as the FDA, EPA, FTC, and FCC are charged with enforcing regulations designed to conform the conduct of the businesses under their jurisdiction. In these instances sometimes public safely is an issue, sometimes the allocation of resources, and sometimes restraint of trade and unfair competition are issues that a regulatory environment seeks to control. There is no question that government has ample resources it may employ in its efforts to control business policy. The tax code, tariffs, allocation of government-owned or controlled resources, and the imposition of a regulatory environment are all tools that the government can, does and is using in the business world today.

The US government is not alone in the world in their regulatory endeavors, and in fact have not gone as far as the governments of some other countries, where entire economic sectors have been nationalized in an effort to bring them under absolute control. American enterprises such as the postal service and Amtrak are virtually government controlled entities, but they are not entirely free from competition, and the profit motive is still a motivating factor in the application of management initiatives applied to problems and opportunities. The ability to succeed or to fail are vital components of American business. There are areas where government regulations are necessary, but when regulations are imposed in an effort to level the playing field and remove the possibility of success or failure, everyone loses.

Sometimes, observers of American business, painting with a very broad brush, opine that "we don't make anything anymore," following that with a discourse on the negative impact of that "fact" on the nation's unemployment rate, the inflation rate, the GNP, and the NYSE. Leaving aside (for a moment) the fact that this premise is not true, we know that all of the indexes claiming to suffer from a decline in manufacturing activity will fluctuate up or down, but to assign a cause-and-effect relationship in advance to any fluctuation is like saying that an inordinate number of butterflies flapping their wings in Guatemala or Myanmar will result in a worse-than-normal hurricane season in Florida. It just may not be true. The butterflies may flap, and the hurricane season may be bad, but did one cause the other? (My apologies here to chaos theorists—I just don't buy it.)

The original statement "we don't make anything anymore" is much too broad to be generally acceptable, but, like many sayings, it contains the seeds of some truth. Technology is allowing us to do more with less in terms of our productive capabilities. The "less" part of the equation seems to impact one factor of production particularly hard, and that factor is human capital.

Henry Ford exploited and perfected the use of human capital in his state-of-the-art automobile factory, and he put the nation on wheels, arguably one of the greatest achievements of the 20th century. We have all seen the pictures—a seemingly endless line of men, each doing his part to assemble the new "American Dream": a Model T Ford. In contrast, look at the production floor of a modern auto plant. It is almost as hard to spot human capital at work as it is to find a clerk (sorry, a "sales associate") at a home improvement store. So, at least as far as cars go, we still do make things, but we make more cars, and better cars, using fewer people to do so. (That may not even be totally true, as we shall see.) The fact is, we make lots of things, and from appliances, to airplanes, to computers, to washing machines, we make more of a better-quality product today than we did last year—maybe even last week—using less human capital and more technology to accomplish the required tasks.

Some businesses have not exploited the tremendous promise and productive potential of today's technology. Why? It is possible that embracing such technology may not help them and may actually have a negative marketing effect on their efforts. Businesses in very mature markets, where personal service is still expected and even necessary, may achieve peak efficiencies with little more than word-processing technology. We do not expect these businesses, mostly service oriented, to achieve productivity gains approaching those in newer market segments by implementing new technology tools. The addition of advanced technology to the enterprise would not justify the required capital expenditures involved. The decision to forego the addition of available technology should be made carefully, with no reliance on decisions made by others, even in similar industry situations.

Nothing we make is really exempt from including human capital in the production equation, and it applies as well to the things we grow. Of course, we are no longer an agrarian society by any stretch of the imagination. Less than 5 percent of American land is used as farms or orchards today, yet we feed not only ourselves, but for some time we also fed nearly half the world's population. We do this so efficiently that the government has found it necessary to provide price supports and crop subsidy payments to our farmers to help them sustain income levels for their production.

Agricultural products, now chiefly produced and distributed through giant farm cooperatives, are one of the more important segments of our working society. Consider the effects of a Midwestern drought or seasonal flooding on our food prices, the inflation rate, and, indeed, the overall economy. While it is unlikely, given modern farming technology, that we would run out of any particular food product or component ingredients, the accompanying price rise due to a shortage could result in a self-imposed price-influenced rationing on the consumption side that would mitigate all but the most severe supply reductions. So, while gardening is the nation's number one outdoor activity, it is not out of necessity that most of us plant and prune, but for the pleasure it gives us to do so.

If the evolution of American business is a success story, it is matched in significance by the evolution of the American farm. Certainly farms do more with less. Remarkable farm machinery has allowed farmers to plant and harvest more with less human involvement, and genetic modifications and other scientific advancements allow for more output of higher-quality goods per acre or per tree. This can be "food for thought" the next time you sit down to a dinner made possible by the bounty of the American farm.

An equally amazing agricultural story is the evolution of the food-processing and distribution system. Many countries can and do grow enough food to feed their citizens, but some of these countries lack the infrastructure, transportation, and distribution systems to process and market the products. The result? Food rots unharvested in the fields, or it is harvested and rots or is eaten by rodents in barns, silos, and warehouses. The net result is what I call "agrarian anomalies," which manifest themselves in activities such as the United States exporting rice to China.

America is not alone in its agricultural prowess. European countries in the EU are competing aggressively in world agricultural markets to export their products. The United States is also sharing its scientific know-how with Third-World countries in an attempt to help them improve the quality of life for their citizens and become somewhat more self-sufficient. Global weather conditions have recently resulted in years-long periods of drought in areas previously agriculturally productive, reducing some to near-desert conditions. These countries need our food, our know-how, and our equipment in order to maximize their output per farm, be it livestock or food products, and we have been happy to provide it to them. In all respects, it's the right thing to do.

If we really do produce and provide "more with less," something must be added to the "less" side of the equation (the human capital side) to make the equation balance. Transfer payments such as state and federal unemployment benefits help to restore a modicum of equilibrium. The concept of "underemployed" has largely disappeared as jobs have inexorably become more complex, but we will always have with us the unemployed and the unemployable. The size of this group as a percentage of the population is a matter of debate. How we deal with this segment of our society is in part a measure of our "goodness" as a civilized people, and in that regard, I am not concerned that these are individuals who will be the forgotten among us. We are at once a strong and a compassionate people, with hard-won freedoms we have enjoyed and employed to create the greatness that is America.

We used to feed and clothe half the world's population, or so it was said. Certainly we did our share. We are speaking past tense here because this statement is no longer true. A relatively new concept is impacting our commercial and industrial empire—the outsourcing of production and services to offshore locations. Also, foreign textile industries have flourished, and as a result, we no longer need to clothe half the world's people. We know, however, that textiles are not really a good example of an outsourced job. Textiles are commodity items that, like televisions and electronics, have been impacted by global competition. Foreign companies now completely produce and assemble many products once considered as "made in the USA." We cannot outsource jobs that we no longer have, or no longer want. We need to do a better job of distinguishing between jobs outsourced and jobs lost. The difference makes a difference.

Technology has reduced, but not eliminated, the need for human capital, and the cost disparities in obtaining the human capital that is required are so great that attractive increases in margins are available to companies that avail themselves of foreign human resources. Other costs, including shipping, scrap, and supervision, may increase, but the overall decrease in wage and fringe costs is more than compensating. Our response to this competition has been both enigmatic and understandable. We have acted as if we have wrung all the efficiencies of production from our technology in these industries; that is the enigmatic part. The understandable part is, assuming that the prior statement is true, we have ceded the production of these products to those producers whose total cost of all factors of production, including human capital, gives them a sustainable competitive advantage, which is the profitable wholesale price of their finished products at a lower cost.

Outsourcing of jobs involves a more aggressive approach by American business, but it also involves the recognition of what is at least a short-term competitive advantage, again involving human capital. Outsourcing jobs to foreign markets is a relatively new concept on the scale in which it is currently being applied. There is no end in sight, and it is a pretty safe assumption that a majority of people who read this know someone who has been affected by foreign outsourcing. What do we mean by "affected"? We mean that co-workers, friends, or relatives have lost their jobs due to foreign competition and U.S. outsourcing of labor-intensive jobs.

It is less expensive for your credit card company to hire someone in India to answer your calls. It is less expensive for your PC manufacturer to troubleshoot your computer's problems from Malaysia. It is less expensive for your auto manufacturer, who over the past decade has forced its suppliers to become more creative in order to deal successfully with razor-thin margins and concurrent increases in quality expectations, to transfer its component assembly work to Mexico. Increased quality problems? Certainly. Difficult and more costly transportation costs? Of course. Customer discontent regarding corporate social responsibility? We are starting to hear it. Wage and benefit disparities are so great, however, that they currently favorably outweigh all the negatives associated with foreign outsourcing.

Workplace observers are quick to point out, true or not, that the outsourcing of production jobs "opens the door" for America to replace the lost jobs with high-paying, clean work in the other sectors of the economy. Retraining of manufacturing workers is a much-discussed topic. What about the welder in his 50s with a 30-year career in manufacturing? What about the press operator who loses his job and simply wants to have a part in the productive process? We cannot allow these workers to do without a job. A job is too much a part of our identity and our self-esteem to do without. A serious discussion on a national scale needs to take place to successfully resolve these types of issues.

How we deal with these issues will have a significant impact on our national character, our national morale, and our national self-esteem. Willing as we might be to subsidize a nonworking lifestyle for the unemployed, the financial consequences of our subsidies do not compensate the unemployed for the loss of status and of self-esteem, and for the productive opportunities that go unfulfilled. The country is also denied the benefits of the unemployed individual's potential contributions to the productive processes in which they might otherwise be involved. Everyone can and should do something, and our best efforts should be directed to making a life of productive pursuits a reality for everyone.

There is another thing that happens when we outsource our production and ask someone else to make our widgets for us: we lose much of our incentive to experiment, to innovate, to try new production methods, and to introduce new technology into the widget-making process. The American spirit of innovation ranks with our patriotism and our entrepreneurial spirit in setting American business apart from and ahead of the rest of the world. We need to nurture that spirit both now and in future generations. We cannot afford to outsource innovation. We should not have to resort to behavior modification by tweaking the tax code to encourage innovation. Innovative entrepreneurship is and has always been a part of the American spirit. It is that freedom-produced creative fire in you and your co-workers. It needs to be encouraged and rewarded in the workplace for America to continue to lead the way.

Outsourcing is a difficult concept with which to deal, but we must. While it is certainly not accurate to proclaim "we don't make anything anymore," we may soon be able to say, with respect to certain industries, we don't make "that" anymore.

Because the economic benefits of foreign outsourcing cannot be ignored, the exodus of production jobs will continue until production price parity is realized. By that point we may well have permanently lost half of the productive capacity of the country. These moves make economic sense for business, but there are social costs as well, which should not be ignored either. We need to make the distinction between the outsourcing of jobs to foreign entities and the concept and the impact of foreign trade. Foreign trade currently has a small but growing impact on our real GDP.

Increasing advancements in technology in foreign manufacturing have resulted in increased competition in the global economy. As a result, foreign-made products, from textiles, to cars, to computers, are sold side by side with U.S.-made goods, all competing for the American consumer's dollar. Recently, foreign trade has also been affected by strong economic growth, which, when it happens in the United States, increases demand for foreign goods. When economic growth in foreign countries accelerates, demand for U.S. goods abroad may increase. Wide swings in foreign trade balances are common as growth in one particular country is under way. It is the trends over time that are cause for concern. Our concern is heightened by our inability, as individuals or even as a community, to manage swings in foreign trade to our benefit.

Another factor that affects foreign trade is the exchange rate. As the dollar's value is strengthened, imports become cheaper and thus more attractive. A combination of reduced inflation and reduced tax rates can stimulate foreign investment in the United States and have the net effect of increasing overall demand for U.S. goods. The pendulum swings both ways however, sometimes with adverse consequences for U.S. business.

At the beginning of this chapter, we spoke about the remarkable job-creating capacity of the American economy. Most recently, we have discussed the diminishing importance of human capital in the manufacturing process. What are we to make of this seeming dichotomy? A good part of the answer lies in the tremendous job-creating growth of the services and professional industries. Despite the explosive growth of services and of professional and intellectual property businesses, many important aspects of these ventures remain enigmatic to us. Most measurements of our productivity, such as output per capita computed in relation to GDP, ROI, and other important ratios and percentages, are relatively easily obtainable in the manufacturing environment. Not so in businesses in which intellectual output or services rendered must somehow be measured.

Additionally, due to the recent emergence of these businesses as well as some of the productivity measurement problems they present, we have not developed a complete "educational set" with respect to success in these activities. Aside from the obvious technical and regulatory knowledge and abilities that must be acquired, what educational experience will maximize a person's chances for success in these fields?

In the last decade, educational institutions and organizations of educators have worked cooperatively with business to make the overall educational process more relevant to each student's future in the world of American business. This has been done in response to business reports of the amount and type of "retraining" that was being undertaken in order to get newly hired employees ready to be productive members of their new organizations. Educational curricula have evolved in response to this information by including team environment problem solving and an increased awareness of the importance of written and verbal communication ability in curriculum course work requirements. The results of these changes have been largely positive. Some would argue that the team approach to problem solving a project to completion has been carried to an extreme. This may be true with respect to some institutions or classes; however, the educational response to business needs has been encouraging to see.

However, an unfortunate development that may be related to some of these changes in the educational process is the attention being given to decreasing individual competition and attempting to increase students' self-esteem in every situation, whether warranted or not, and often regardless of the academic effort being put forth. While this subject is beyond the scope of our discussion, suffice it to say that, in our schools, academic rigor needs to be rewarded, and those who strive and achieve should be rewarded and recognized—not as "geeks" or "nerds," but as high achievers worthy of respect. It would not be unwise for all of our clamoring for educational reform to include a renewed emphasis on gaining knowledge and rewarding those who succeed, while encouraging those who put forth the effort.

Recall our earlier praise of Henry Ford in successfully implementing the mass production manufacturing process in the United States. Recall also our assumption that today's automobile production is accomplished with fewer workers, allowing for the possibility that that may not, in fact, be a true statement. A mitigating factor to the "fewer workers" statement is the reallocation of manpower from the non-automated production process to other areas of the business that require increased attention. Henry Ford's mass production workforce consisted primarily of auto assembly workers, all men. Today, Mr. Ford's company produces far more cars per day, but the human workforce consists primarily of IT departments, accountants, engineers, research departments, robotic technicians, and delivery and clerical personnel, both men and women. Many observers in fact believe that it is precisely the growth of these ancillary jobs in old-line companies that has facilitated women's entry into the workforce.

Today, there is every reason to believe that service, technology, and other intellectual pursuits will continue to increase in their importance and will continue to evolve in response to needs and abilities manifested by new and improving technology. They will be the subject of much debate and analysis and will, to a greater and greater extent, be the drivers of our economy. So now, let's turn our attention to various aspects of American business for a closer look at what makes a business venture successful in today's complex environment.

The following chapters are certainly not meant to be an exhaustive analysis of each subject discussed, but rather a springboard for group discussion as well as for individual thought. Our corporate culture is defined by looking at what we have put in place to direct, measure, and control the actions of ourselves and of others who are helping us to achieve our corporate goals. All these concepts are important to us. If they are not, they should be discarded, or they should be amended until they provide an efficient paradigm for the way corporate America achieves success.

MANAGEMENT = LEADERSHIP

"A leader must be honest with himself and know
that as a leader he is just like everybody else. He
must identify himself with the group. He must back
up the group, even at the risk of displeasing
superiors. He must believe that the group wants
from him a sense of approval. If this feeling
prevails, production, discipline, morale will be
high, and in return, you can demand the
cooperation to promote the goals of the company."
—Vincent Lombardi

The American Heritage Dictionary is remarkably unhelpful in aiding one to understand the definition of *management*. The definition reads, in relevant part, "executive ability" and "the act, manner, or practice of managing." The definition of *manager* is equally enlightening, being "one who manages." Insight arrives when we get to the word *manage*: "To direct, control, or handle. To administer or regulate. To make submissive. To continue or arrange."

It should not be lost on the reader that the most helpful definition is found under the verb *manage*—not the nouns *management* or *manager*. To manage implies action, cognitive and physical. *Roget's Thesaurus* includes among its *manage* synonyms (as a verb): *administer, care for, boss, command, dominate, officiate, rule, run, steer, supervise, train, watch over,* and *direct*.

Hundreds of books, many of them best sellers, have been written and sold on the "art" of management. Common ideas are sometimes hard to identify among these authors. (Think for a moment about the assignment of the word *art* to the act of managing, versus the assignment of the word *practice* to the act of accounting, and you will get a sense of the expansive dynamics of management versus the restrictive regulations of accounting.)

We could devote the balance of this chapter to a definition of *management* (we use it as a verb in most instances), but we are, for purposes of this discussion, going to set forth a definition that will allow us to go on. Management is leadership, and all that leadership entails.

With so many ideas in the corporate world about the role and definition of management and managers, it is important that we start from a common point—agreeing that management is synonymous with leadership will help establish our initial point of agreement.

More about the books on management. Virtually none are without some merit, however disparate their policies and procedures may be. This is a testimony to the dynamic nature of the management process. It also attests to the sensitivity of management practice to the existing or evolving corporate culture. Books on management and corporate leadership by such luminaries as Peter Drucker and Jack Welch, to name only two, are, or should be, on every manager's "must read" list. If someone like Jack Welch is willing to write and sell a book to share with others what he has learned about leadership during his remarkable tenure at General Electric, I cannot conceive of a rational reason why every manager in every business would not read that book, and why appropriate implementation of his ideas would not go far to assure a going concern's success. A majority of successful managers are avid readers.

Fortunately or unfortunately, most management policies, procedures, and philosophies do not come from a book. They are the products of successful directed effort by leaders of an enterprise. It is not unusual, as a business grows and management layers are added, to have the company's founder as its chairman, or its CEO, sometimes for many years. Since all companies eventually sell either a product or a service, the focus of the CEO must be expansive and shift in intensity and focus to areas of most concern at the time. If our founder/CEO is so because he or she is the engineer who invented the product or the process the company was set up to sell, he or she may be hindered by a lack of knowledge about marketing, uninterested in accounting, and filled with anxiety about growth and change. These traits may be in part responsible for the focus that led the engineer to success as an inventor or innovator, but they could spell doom for the company unless our founder/CEO recognizes his or her shortcomings and surrounds himself or herself with good people who may know very little about inventing but a lot about marketing, accounting, and corporate growth and change.

Is it proper to refer to a supervisor as a manager? When properly used, the term "supervisor" in most corporate settings is a job title for an individual whose duties would not carry with them the weight of accountability equal to a manager's. Supervisors typically direct the activities of others in order to successfully and efficiently achieve the manager's or the company's goals. The manager of a business, not unlike the head coach or manager of a professional sports team, is responsible for actual achievement and will be judged on the results of each initiative, not always fairly, but judged against the one unrelenting criterion—expectations.

If management is leadership, there must obviously be people to lead. In a majority of instances, there is a direct relationship between the quality of the leadership and the quality of the results of that leadership. In some circumstances, exceptional employees can produce results that make the average manager look better than average. In some circumstances, the surrounding corporate culture can contribute intangible motivation that will positively impact the outcome of an operation. Either one of these situations can work to increase a manager's odds of beating the Peter Principle, but in most cases, only quality leadership begets quality results.

Because supervisors are, in most instances, the last layer of "nonmanagement" to be added to the corporate organization, most often a manager will be managing (read "leading") a group of supervisory-level employees toward specific common goals. Whether managing hourly employees or other managers or supervisors, the manager's job is the same. How the manager goes about it will both determine and be determined by his or her management skills and the corporate culture in which the skills are employed.

There are a wide variety of management styles that are employed to varying degrees and with varying results across the corporate landscape. Newly minted or newly promoted managers would do well to assess the existing corporate culture for clues to adopting a successful management persona. Attempting to manage by inserting a rigid management style that is at variance with the prevailing corporate culture is an effort fraught with pitfalls, and most probably headed for the headlines—in a B-school case-study textbook.

Writing on the subject of management needs to be read and understood in light of this fact: the successful employment of a management style is in reality the successful employment of a combination of management skills which, taken together, successfully combine with other incentivising elements of the existing corporate culture to produce successfully managed outcomes. If someone decides to provide a name for his or her management style, such as "Management by Objective" or "Management by Walking Around" or "Absentee Management," that person should not assume that each aspect of that management style can or should be integrated into his or her particular management situations. The best managers pick and choose management styles and skills, employing those that fit the time, place, people, and objective.

You're getting results, maintaining corporate values and moral and ethical standards, but you can't label your management style? Good for you. Create your own label if it's important to you to do so, but don't be afraid to change with the times and the circumstances.

With so much attention paid to management style, there are inherent within these styles some management skills that are present in most successful managers' résumés. These skills are what are deserving of attention. They should be considered à la carte and used as the entrée, appetizer, or garnish, depending on the circumstances, the culture, and the expectations. Here in brief are some of the skills managers should have to manage (remember: manage = lead) successfully:

Leadership ability. A manager should (be able to) command respect. Perhaps the operative word here, speaking in the corporate sense, is *command*. Respect is acquired in a combination of ways as the manager-managed relationship develops, but "commanding" respect is actually the act of being respected as a result of having earned respect by virtue of management performance, managed results, and successful employee relationships. This type of respect is the most rewarding, most enduring, and most productive of all types. Respect that is accorded by virtue of an individual's title, connections, or time on the job certainly exists but lacks value in directing employee activity and producing results, as does fear-based respect.

Leadership enjoyment. A manager should enjoy his or her job. This may seem like an overly obvious qualification, and perhaps it is. What is meant by this statement, however, is that a manager should enjoy all that the manager's job entails. Chief among these is accountability for results. Enjoyment of accountability comes from confidence in one's role as a manager and confidence in corporate objectives and management's role in attaining those objectives. When objectives are being discussed as just that—objectives—that is the time to assess the objectives' value and how best to attain them. "Objectives" passing the first stage become "expectations," and pass from there to become "results."

If management objectives are clear and concise (i.e., are the stated objectives the real objectives?), if they make business and economic sense, if they fall within the corporate value system, and if the corporate culture has equipped you with the tools you need to accomplish your part (authority, mentoring, budgeting), then you should receive enjoyment from the challenge and the resultant praise or punishment. Other aspects of the job, including possible travel, long days, intellectual challenges, and unreasonable expectations should also be enjoyable challenges of the job, or "managed" into an enjoyable status.

Leadership by example—walking the walk. Nowhere in business is the management-employee relationship as structured as it is in the branches of the U.S. military. It is most often in a military context that we hear: "Don't ask your men to do something you would not do yourself." This phrase can apply in the corporate world as well. A charismatic, can-do attitude on the manager's part will do much to energize and focus those whom you depend upon to help achieve the set objectives (now the expectations). Empathy has its place as well, to a point. Proper introduction of empathy into the process requires a clear understanding of each team member's job. Each employee tends to think of his or her job as the indispensable part of the equation.

Empathy with employees' positions may be important in needed motivation, as long as the empathy does not lead to pity or patronization. Summarized, this means that the pursuit of the objective itself should be enjoyable, though challenging. Learn to say "we" when speaking about performance and goal achievement.

Adopting the "management horizon." Management's focus—it's "horizon"—is necessarily more long term and far-reaching than the horizon of the managed team. Generally speaking, as a company grows, so does its bureaucracy and its management layers, and as non-management employees' jobs become more specific and compartmentalized, so does their job horizon.

Non-management employees are task-oriented. The manager's job is to direct and focus those present-day tasks in such a way as to achieve long-term results. Six-month results mean very little to the employee who is trying to decide where to have lunch that day. One of a manager's most difficult tasks is to translate day-to-day activities into the action plans that will achieve the long-term objectives in an effective way and vice versa. The rewards for success—satisfaction, recognition, respect, and responsibility—should be welcomed and enjoyed by those who have earned it, and shared with those who contributed to the effort.

"Team Player" attitude. Attitudes are an important barometer of progress and of ultimate success. Good managers are team players both with fellow managers and with employees under their purview or on their "team." Team player attitudes with employees under supervision by a manager call for a delicate balance, hopefully to be nurtured by an open, inclusive corporate culture. Being a team player is not being "one of the guys," and, at the same time, it is not distancing oneself from the team via a manager's persona, or attitude, carried to an extreme.

Good managers are good listeners, aware that their employees have good ideas that deserve a hearing and subsequent implementation, or valid reasons for not adopting a suggested idea. There is no surer way to get employees to buy into a plan than to give them some say in how to achieve the objective. If an employee's idea is implemented and makes the manager's efforts more successful, proper management of the process is crucial to assure that an employee's good idea makes everyone look good. The very best and most noble plans will suffer when implementation is undertaken by disheartened employees with confusing or conflicting ideas about the objectives and how they are to be achieved. How much of this picture is the fault of the manager in charge? In the harsh world of corporate expectations: all of it.

Good managers are also good communicators who enjoy and recognize the importance of keeping their employees up-to-date on relevant progress in meeting goals, which also have been shared with the employees in a manner that relates to the jobs they do. Good news, bad news, praise, punishment, setbacks, and successes all need to be shared cogently and not condescendingly with employees who have a stake in the outcome.

A good manager is a team player on the management team as well. Here again, being a good listener and a good communicator are vital skills of good managers. Thoughtful input on goals, objectives, and action plans, doing your homework on the issues and disagreeing without being disagreeable would make you, as manager, a valued member of the team. As a rule, managers should not expose a problem without also proposing a solution, especially in a one-on-one meeting. A good manager will have balanced ambitions, being realistic about his or her personal future at the company. While it is good to have a plan, it is important to assure that your plans involve maintaining corporate values and ethics, even in a crisis situation. Suggesting and implementing successful contingency plans will earn most managers a gold star in that infamous "permanent file." Curb your ego; be willing to learn and to teach effectively.

While a senior management position is the end of the rainbow for many, not all are driven to this goal. Some of the most effective and valuable employees in a company are those whose experience in and attitude about their current positions places them exactly where they want to be. Want to reward that top salesperson? Don't necessarily make him or her the next sales manager. Unhappy with administrative duties, unmotivated with a commission-less salary, and unimpressed with a corner office, a top salesperson now lacks those aspects of the job that were so important to his or her initial success. Couple this with undoubtedly outsized corporate expectations, no mentoring, and the learning curve for the replacement salesman, and the whole company pays a price for misplaced administration.

Successful promotions to management positions require that management skills be quickly learned and effectively applied—not an easy step for an otherwise motivated performer who may actually be resentful of and threatened by the demands and expectations now being put upon him or her by virtue of the promotion.

However, if the salesman has the desire and perceived aptitude and attitude for the management position, then consideration of such a move may be in order. As with all promotions that "automatically" go to the best performers, the learning curves must be taken into account. If you have a good thing going, try to make it work.

It is common for a manager's financial compensation in to be in the form of a salary rather than hourly remuneration. With the possible exception of very senior-level executives, the salaries of managers in publicly-held companies are not published for all the world to see and discuss. A middle manager's salary should be sufficient to recognize the effort and time required, and the importance of the expected results. Companies utilizing all kinds of salary scales for management level employees are often taking the easy way out. Financial bracketing will not mitigate the efforts of most managers—see the chapter on motivation—but it will not financially distinguish good or bad efforts from the average. Is your company too big to monitor the jobs being done by all those managers? Oops! Time for some administrative quality control, which, it seems, inevitably turns into administrative quantity control. Salary increases should be commensurate with increased responsibilities and increased expectations. The super-sized, ridiculous salaries and bonuses paid to major corporate chieftains may be the "brass ring" for some, but the reality for most managers is a financial future which, with adequate planning and no unanticipated occurrences, can be comfortable and relatively secure.

If you believe you deserve to be paid more than "the chart" says, or more than you have been offered, tell someone about it. You will get a response—to a lot of questions, such as:

> How valuable am I in my supervisor's eyes?
> Does the person responsible for determining my financial future
>   evaluate me—or does someone else?
> What am I doing right?
> What am I doing wrong?
> Does this "answer" help me plan my future more accurately?
> Is what I do important to the company?
> Am I adequately appreciated, financially and in other ways?
> Do I have a future with this company?
> What can I do better?

How managers in positions similar to yours at another company are doing financially is information that should be readily accessible through your network of associates. Remember, your paycheck is just that, and as important as that may be, it is only one component of your overall career package. Many other aspects of your job, tangible and intangible, need to be considered in order to answer important career questions.

It can be said that those who desire to be known by their peers as "good managers" and who apply their skills and knowledge to achieve that goal will, in the process, learn life leadership lessons that benefit them not only in their business careers, but in virtually all aspects of their lives and lifestyles. That's a win-win endeavor.

MISSION

"I demand a commitment to excellence and
to victory and that is what life is all about."
—Vincent Lombardi

How many goals does your company have today? Is the answer to this question reduced down to a "Things to do" list of short-term projects? Not to pick on lists: there is much to be said for creating a daily or a weekly prioritized projects list from which to work. Short-term goals are the real driving force in any company on an individual level. The real key is to be sure, without asking everyone, that the individual goals all contribute in some positive way to the overall goals of the company.

Goals, to be effective, must be clearly defined and achievable, among other things. Clearly defined goals are, in corporate America, usually short-term goals, due to the volatile, extraneous forces being exerted on our organizations in a dynamic free-market economy. Are these your typical goals?

- The financials simply must be completed by mid-week.
- Action plans need to be created and critiqued for the next planning meeting.
- New product review is long overdue, and the sales department is screaming for new computers.
- The briefcase will be full tonight.

Is this a good list or a bad list? Is there such a thing as a good or bad list if the goals are all under your control? Can a manager be too goal-driven?

Goals are the lifeblood of the motivated self-starter. Give that person a goal and step out of the way. Just as the goals of individual employees must all contribute to the goals of the company, the company goals all must make a positive contribution to the overall mission of the corporation. This needs to happen by virtue of a clean and consistent mission, without constant oversight and monitoring.

If you are unfamiliar with a mission statement, here is a quick primer. Usually several sentences in length, and seldom shorter than two or longer than five, a mission statement is the elucidation of a company's overall objective. The objective is not an achievable "then we rest" objective, but rather one that the company believes needs to be achieved on an ongoing basis in order for the business to be defined as a successful going concern. A mission statement rarely speaks of profitability, but many speak much about adding value and exceeding customers' expectations.

What is the mission of your company? Is it to make as much money as possible? To be socially responsible? Does your mission incorporate traditionally accepted values? Does it need to? What do you expect a mission statement to do? Is it stated? Do you even need one?

The mission statement should be composed, very carefully, by the management team that runs the company. Members of this team have, by their collective management styles, defined the corporate culture and have set the corporate goals. The team may want to have the statement objectively critiqued by an outside consultant, but the theme and the tone need to fit with the existing corporate culture for the statement to be effective. What you have at this point is a mission statement that maybe six to 10 people have read and who understand what it means. What you need to avoid next is to have a mission statement that everyone in the company has read, but only six to 10 people understand.

Consider for a moment how remarkable it is that tens, hundreds, even thousands of people can come together each day and, by effectively doing their jobs, contribute to the overall success of a business enterprise. How often do we discuss "focus" and "corporate objectives" with those assigned to achieve those objectives? Not very often. Management's objectives are (or should be) longer-term and more comprehensive as we move up the bureaucratic ladder. Companies that produce a single product, many products, or no products would be very different from each other in their evolution, their structure, and the managers' jobs associated with each one. All successful businesses, however, find common ground in a remarkable ability to organize, collaborate, and integrate in order to achieve their goals. The ability to do this consistently depends on an abundance of entrepreneurial spirit and free-market economics—Adam Smith's invisible hand at work.

The opportunity to state and discuss a company's overall objectives, its raison d'être, is one that should not be overlooked. Amazing as it may be to look at what businesses have been able to accomplish without giving a corporate mission statement a thought, it is not hard to imagine that more could have been achieved, or equal success with fewer missteps, by the introduction of a properly phrased and properly presented mission statement, one that is understandable, defensible, and honorable.

As important as the preparation phase is, the presentation phase can make or break the mission statement's effectiveness. Many of us have experienced the "mission statement moment" at work. Shortly after returning from a weeklong management retreat and submitting properly completed expense reports for expensive meals, dreamed-of greens fees, and exorbitant sundry supplies, the powers that be call a corporate-wide meeting. This meeting is usually held at 5:05 P.M. so as to minimize any interruption in productivity and maximize rush-hour miseries. The purpose of the meeting quickly becomes apparent—a corporate "mission statement" (hopefully, the company's first rather than a revised one) has been adopted and is now to be imparted to the rank and file.

Typically, a mission statement consists of several adjective and verb-laden sentences espousing the founding purpose of the company. It is first read, then unveiled on a plaque in the lunch room, and, for a good measure, given to each employee on a laminated card at the end of the meeting and enclosed with the employee's next paycheck. The employees shuffle home or back to work, and business resumes as usual.

We make light here of the mission statement moment, but, sadly, it is also a pretty accurate account of what takes place at many businesses.

Instead, the statement should initially be presented by one of its authors to a group of workers who have similar or common functions within the company. Production, accounting, marketing, etc., each gets its own meeting. A small company could successfully present the statement at a single meeting. The purpose of the departmental presentation is to provide the opportunity to explain the statement in a way that is meaningful to each individual. The explanation to the accounting department of how its efforts contribute to the overall accomplishment of the mission statement will differ significantly from the discussion you hold with the production group, or engineering, marketing, or any other department.

While the discussion can and should involve a give-and-take dialogue, changing or amending the statement is not a discussion item. Careful preparation of the statement will result in one that is comprehensive and effective enough to serve the company well for many years. Employees should understand that this is an important statement that contains information that management considers essential to the overall success of the company. Unless your existing corporate culture so dictates, however, the presentation of the statement should not be accomplished with great pomp and circumstance.

Obviously, management needs to speak with a single voice regarding the meaning of the mission statement. The statement should be incorporated as page one of the employee's handbook. It should be reproduced as a poster and displayed in a common meeting area, such as a break room, entryway, or a common hallway. If your building has a lobby, it can also be displayed for customers and visitors to read.

A word about posters: most of the "attitude" posters that are so popular today are very appropriate for business settings of all types. They are aesthetically pleasing with a positive, encouraging message that is general enough in content that the message would not be confused with, or in conflict with, the mission statement message. If your corporate culture allows for and encourages creativity, these posters can be displayed beside a whiteboard with erasable markers. As employees think about the poster's message, they can compose their own creative thoughts for all to see. Signed or unsigned, these comments often are clever and thought provoking in their own right.

Most mission statements are clearly worded as to the company's mission which, broadly speaking, is a summation of the company's overall business objective. Discussion items appropriate for mission statement analysis include the goals that must be met in order to achieve the objective, a time frame in which to achieve the goals, and a plan for maintaining the company's focus in order to achieve and maintain it's mission objective. Strategic planning is the breakdown of these broadly stated goals and objectives into manageable action plans, including timing deadlines and accountability assignments. A properly drafted, inspiring mission statement helps your employees validate their efforts and can provide the basis for many valuable decision making discussions.

A mission statement can be as valuable as you make it, so make the most of it. Its introduction into the workplace can provide valuable focus (or refocus) of your precious corporate resources: time, people, and money. Properly prepared and presented, it can be a unifying document that adds vitality and purpose to your employees' efforts.

MONEY

"To achieve success, whatever the job we
have, we must pay a price. Success is
like anything worthwhile. It has a price. You have to
pay the price to win and you have to
pay the price to get to the point where
success is possible. Most important, you
must pay the price to stay there."
—Vincent Lombardi

The cliché that "money is the lifeblood of the company" is an analogy that works on several different levels when comparing it to the blood that circulates in our bodies. Number one, it is a true statement; number two, there are different types (currencies); number three, there is a "universal donor" (U.S. dollars); number four, an injury to either body or company can cause it to "bleed"; and number five, both blood and money are stored in banks. (Clichés, like comedy, make sense only if they contain an element of truth.)

While there are a number of corporate functions that seem far removed from the "bean counter's" disciplines, none can escape the financial or accounting department's relentless scrutiny. (Although there can be a difference between a financial department and an accounting department, for our purposes, the terms will be used interchangeably.) There is no question that it is an absolutely indispensable administrative function. In a publicly held company, the accounting department would be responsible for calculating monthly, quarterly, or even weekly sales margin and profit numbers, whose publication will affect the price of a company's stock.

The use of short-term numbers as a stock-price driver is, of course, ridiculous, and its utilization in such a way prompts corporate controllers and CFOs to assume, shall we say, sometimes "obtuse" accounting policies, in an effort to meet analysts' expectations for their company for a particular month, quarter, or season. WorldCom and Enron-type debacles have resulted in the imprisonment of CEOs and CFOs who have been convicted of abusing the use of accounting statements to veil the true operating condition of their companies—and abuse of a public trust that investors have, perhaps mistakenly, put in corporate management.

Corporate analysts' expectations are relentless, and mitigating circumstances are seldom sufficiently acknowledged in analyzing results. In times of crisis, suddenly the accounting policies and those who administrate them within the organization become the center of (unwanted) attention.

This is not to say that proper financial administration is an easy follow-the-rules task. Within the purview of generally accepted accounting principles, it is hard enough to encompass various treatments of income and expense items, and companies that are hard pressed to "hit the numbers" will look to book accounting entries in a way that best suits their current situation. Although highly regulated, companies often find the creative wiggle room necessary to satisfy their needs.

The accounting department often develops relatively late in the company's early life and is often born of necessity. Another administrative, nonproductive layer of overhead and oversight, setting forth policies and procedures, expense reports and deadlines—just what a growing, dynamic, on-the-go company needs, right? Well, sometimes it is exactly what the company needs.

An accounting department's evolution can have a huge impact on the development of the company's corporate culture. A typical financial department begins with a bookkeeper who accumulates data, often then transferring the data to an outside accounting firm for compilation into financial statements and financial management reports for the company's use. The bookkeeper also pays the bills and makes deposits, calls on delinquent accounts, prepares the payroll, and pays the related taxes. Ancillary key functions are identified and assigned to other personnel or to the outside accountant. Tasks such as monthly reconciliation of the bank account and signing checks are often jobs performed by others, thereby decreasing the likelihood of the occurrence of financial fraud by increasing the likelihood of its detection at an early stage because of the separation of duties.

The addition to the staff of an accountant rather than or in addition to a bookkeeper is a significant one, and his or her personality will certainly be a contributing factor to the overall corporate personality, or culture. It would not be unwise, when seeking a corporate accountant, to consider the applicant's potential to grow with the company, even eventually to assume the position of CFO at the appropriate time. Accounting disciplines seem particularly sensitive to change, and a change in personnel is no exception. Unnecessary changes and additions are, of course, the exceptions to the rule.

The nature and the rigors of corporate accounting require a systematic, orderly department, which is often best run by a deadline-driven, results-oriented individual who possesses a high degree of technical ability, coupled with unquestionable integrity and ethical standards. It is not uncommon for the personality and culture of the financial department to be seemingly at odds with the overall culture of a forward-looking, dynamic, on-the-move organization. Every effort should be made to accommodate and welcome the department's discipline. Its job is unique in the business world. At times, input from other departments is welcomed (such as at budget time), and at other times it is not. The department members' work is meaningful and specific, and the language of finance is as beautiful to them as it is baffling to us.

It is an unfortunate fact that a department that can be so proactive is so often in the corporate spotlight being reactive; times of financial crisis have everyone asking "Why?"—a question that could have been avoided if the right question had been asked earlier: "What if . . . ?"

The financial department's abilities and input are limited only by others' expectations. Members of the department can tell you how much that new machine will cost, and, if you ask, they can tell you how much more it is going to cost for the insurance, maintenance, and manpower required to run that new piece of machinery. They can also tell you how much you could have saved if you had leased that new piece of machinery, and they can even tell you how much more you would have saved by outsourcing that entire productive process to another company.

That a company's financial department is often overlooked is not surprising. It is not likely that the company's founder was an accountant (unless the company is an accounting firm), but rather an inventor or an investor. It is likely that the company's accounting/ financial department was added hesitantly, and maybe even begrudgingly. In the search for corporate talent and management prospects, an exceptional person from the financial area may be noticed and evaluated, but history tells us that those most likely to rise to the top do so from within the operation and marketing departments. The greatest mistake that businesses make with regard to their financial department personnel is to consistently underestimate their abilities and the failure to use their work product (i.e., "the numbers") in productive and valuable ways.

The bedrock function of any company's financial department is to crunch the numbers. The income and expenditures of the company over a specific period of time are categorized and put into financial statement form. At certain times, this information is made available to management, sometimes edited or recast for internal company use in management report format.

If the company's stock is publicly or widely held, then statements are usually published in report form, together with the auditor's comments and footnotes. Corporate audit engagements involve relatively intensive scrutiny of the company's financial transactions, how these transactions are categorized, and the verification of account balances. An auditor's footnotes will often give the auditor's opinion of the effect of certain transactions, contract performance, or litigation issues on the current and future financial conditions of the company. A comprehensive financial audit is considered to be the best assurance available that the company is presenting an honest financial report.

Two other types of reports, a review and a compilation, do not subject the records to the type of scrutiny that an audit does. As we have recently seen, however, even an audit performed by a major auditing firm, costing millions of dollars, is no guarantee that financial fraud is not being committed. How transactions are booked may seem to be an issue that is not negotiable, but such is not the case. When a company such as Enron is discovered to be not just unhealthy financially, but functionally insolvent, in spite of audited statements to the contrary, the guilty suffer and so do those charged with an audit that should have brought questionable accounting policies to light and to a resolution.

While an outside firm's audit of your books is not a guarantee, it is usually a very good idea. The engagement can be expensive and can often lead to some relationship issues due to honest differences of opinion as the audit progresses, but most who go through the process are happy that they did and feel better informed as a result.

An extensive, well-conducted audit will not necessarily be confined to the operations within the financial department. It may touch upon and explore operations in a number of different departments for purposes of assuring compliance and accuracy when it comes to "the numbers." The financial department, however, has the final say as to the timing and placement of income and expenses, and is looked to for final accountability.

An unfortunate reason for the underutilization of the financial department's information is the surprising inability of many managers to read a financial statement and come away with any useful information. We are not going to subject readers to a tutorial on financial statement analysis, but it is a bit of mystery why numbers, which can suddenly become so important at a time of crisis, are routinely tossed aside by people who, with a little effort, could almost always find some information in their company's financial statement that they could put to constructive use.

Here is a very brief overview that may be helpful in getting started, but there is no substitute for sitting down with a statement, and maybe with someone from the accounting department, and learning what the numbers are trying to tell you. Here are some things to look for:

1. Balance sheet—A summary of what the company owns (assets), such as cash, securities, inventory, and machinery and office equipment, and what the company owes (liabilities), such as unpaid bills, notes, and loans payable. The difference between the two is the company's equity—usually a positive number.
2. Income statement (profit and loss statement)—A summary of how much money was made (sales, income, revenue), and how much it cost to make that money, categorized by type of expense, such as cost of materials, labor, utilities, taxes, interest on debt, etc. The difference is net income or net loss—hopefully, a positive number.
3. Statement of cash flows—A summary of where the money comes from, such as operating income, new bank loans, sale of stock, sale of assets, and where the money went, such as paying bills, buying new equipment, paying off loans or notes, buying back company stock, or paying dividends.

Numbers from these statements can be used to calculate ratios that help determine how your company is doing in efficiently employing its assets. Comparative statements prepared on a monthly or annual basis help to determine if growth is occurring, whether it is being achieved by price or volume changes, and whether the related costs are being kept in line. A company really needs to know if each new dollar in sales last year cost $1.05 to achieve. Comparatives are also useful in identifying trends, in enabling you to take action before more serious problems occur, or in building upon emerging successes.

There are many valuable things the numbers tell us. All else being equal, wiser is the manager who can interpret a breakeven analysis chart, for example, and glean from it some information that is useful to him or her, and wiser still is the manager who can do his or her own breakeven and other ratios that are proven tools for spotting trends for the benefit of the manager's own department or the company as a whole.

Your financial people can provide more than just financial compliance. Use the information they can provide to make better financial decisions. Choices such as whether to make or buy, to lease or own, or to add the capability to add new production can all be made easier with the type of information the financial department can provide. Expect the department members, as a routine part of their job, to be able to provide you with financial projections based on what-if scenarios, risk analysis, and tax consequences of various courses of action. Wise use of this overhead-increasing department's abilities could easily save you the cost of having such a department each year.

Don't miss the opportunities that exist simply because they may be presented in a format that is not familiar to you. Ask for a written narrative to accompany the financials, or ask for a management report highlighting the more significant numbers and presenting comparative totals, trends, and ratios that are important to running your business more intelligently and efficiently. Ask yourself, "What would I like to know about my company's financial condition and its financial future?" Then go and find the answers.

Don't expect bombastic risk-takers in your financial department. Expect and admire their orderly, uncompromising world. When it comes to "the numbers," intolerance of error is a blessing. Ask tough questions; demand quick, honest answers. A financial crisis is only unforeseen if the warning signs are ignored. The current corporate landscape is littered with the personal tragedies resulting from those "unforeseen financial crises." In such times, people will sometimes be calmed and reassured by only one thing: "Show me the money!"

MARKETING

"A man who is trained to his peak capacity
will gain confidence. Confidence is contagious and so is lack
of confidence and a customer will recognize both."
—Vincent Lombardi

If, as we said, money is the lifeblood of the organization, then marketing must be the heart. (We could complete the organizational anatomy metaphor by classifying management as the brains—thereby possibly giving some managers far too much credit—actual production or provision of services as the hands, motivation as the feet, and the all-encompassing corporate culture as the soul of the organization.) Like the other subjects outlined in this book, the subject of organizational marketing is far too broad to be exhaustively analyzed but also far too important to ignore. "Proper" or "effective" marketing will bring to bear all other elements of our corporate culture in proper and abundant mix to produce the desired results, which are themselves important in assuming the continued success of the business.

A corporate marketing function typically evolves as a separate department early in a company's formation. Data points indicating a company's financial successes or failures will usually be coincident with marketing department successes or failures. Like other corporate departments, there are many marketing mistakes, which, if not addressed promptly, can cause situations that can threaten the very existence of the company or the carefully built and tended reputation of the company and its products or services.

Marketing without market research does not exist. What does exist is marketing that is promoted as market research. While a company can get lucky and develop and promote a new product or service that is immediately well received, that company stands as the exception to the rule. While market research is required to a greater or lesser degree preceding new product or service rollout, the time, amount, cost, and nature of the research itself are all a vital component of the mix. The corporate landscape is rife with corporate skeletons representing companies with good product or service concepts that were re-engineered and/or researched ad nauseam, burning cash that was not replaced with income from product or service sales.

Marketing genius Microsoft participates in market research, customer test sites, and product marketing at its highest level, but there is an active patch program—a problem-solving program that figures out "bugs"—that exists for years-old Microsoft operating systems. Certainly market research and the pursuit of product or service perfection can, and should, continue after the product's or service's introduction, but such research should be funded, at least in part, by revenues from sales of the product or service or by knowingly subsidizing the research using revenue streams from other products or services.

In this section, we will use the word *product* to refer to tangible property manufactured or otherwise acquired and sold, as well as to services developed and sold, because the concepts apply to both.

Most products are born of need, affirming the cliché "necessity is the mother of invention." This cliché, however, is not as true today as it was in earlier times when inventions truly were necessities (e.g., the wheel). It is doubtful that the wheel, the spoon, or the fig leaf was subjected to much market research. These items were used and modified over the years to become what they are today. While some items are subject to heavy modification, others seem to suit their users virtually unchanged from their original form. For example, in a field as active as medical technology, two of the most commonly used medical instruments, the thermometer and the stethoscope, exist today in a form that would be recognizable to their inventors of long ago.

Two bedrock marketing truisms are in play in the modern marketplace:

1) Unless you have invented the marketable equivalent of the wheel, some market research is probably in order, and
2) Just because there is a product on the market that adequately serves a need does not mean there is not a market for your product that serves the same need. (How many "better mousetraps" are out there?)

Unless your product is of a complex nature, its advantages or the need it fills will be apparent to its intended (target) market. That is where most market research can begin. This research should include accumulating data that will help to answer the following questions:

- Who wants my product? (What is my marketplace?)
- Who are my competitors?
- What advantages do I have over my competitors?
- What modifications would make my product better?
- Are those modifications possible to make cost-effectively?
- Does my product provide me with a sustainable competitive advantage in the marketplace?
- If there are no competitive products, how likely is it that they will soon appear? (For example, effective competition is less likely if there is a high initial capital cost required for market entry or there are regulating roadblocks.)
- What price do I have to charge for my product to make a profit?
- What is the market willing to pay for my product?
- What is the most effective way to market my product?
- What are other ways to market my product?
- What advantages does my product have that I can exploit in my marketing approach?
- What advantages does our company have over others that I can exploit in my marketing approach? (For example, corporate name recognition, quality reputation, price reputation).
- Is this a cool breakthrough product that needs to go to market now, doing market research "on the fly"?

Only when these questions are answered to the company's satisfaction should product introduction be planned. Effective marketing of your company's product is a vital job—absolutely essential to the company's survival. All corporate disciplines can take some credit for effective marketing strategies. In today's global (and knowledgeable) marketplace, your product must be produced right, priced right, and presented right, in order to be successful.

To this point we have focused extensively on marketing activities that have to do with market research and product introduction. To end our marketing discussion at this point would be to overlook several significant marketing facts. For example, product costs need to be closely monitored. In today's marketplace, the acquisition and storage of inventory sometimes results in costs that reflect the opposite of what one would expect from "traditional" economic models. "Just in time" and other similar inventory control methods have shifted much of the inventory storage costs further down the line, while incessant advances in technology result in price reductions in product components over time, rather than inflation-driven price increases. Price decreases in product component costs are not uncommon, as companies benefit from increased production volumes and technology-assisted efficiencies.

However, component costs can go the other direction as well, sometimes for reasons beyond the producer's control. Increased demand for a key raw material may precipitate a price increase that must be passed on to the component or product buyer. Global material and product demands and global production costs also play a part in pricing decisions. Inattention to your product prices and costs of production (i.e., your margin) could result in a competitive advantage, based on price, being transferred to a competitor who is exploiting falling component costs, superior inventory control methods, or technology-driven production efficiencies.

Attention must also be paid to product life cycles. In today's market, a mature product may be months old, rather than years. And the resultant competition to a successful product can accelerate your product's perceived demise. Some companies can successfully exploit the "we were first" concept. For those that cannot, shortened life cycles reinforce the need for careful market research, constant product improvement, and careful budgeting. For instance, marketing's advertising budget must often be increased even after an initial marketing "blitz," due to a direct competitor's product introductions. In a marketplace where even the most innovative products can quickly become commodity items, the concept of product loyalty is as outdated as yesterday's laptop. If your product's sustainable competitive advantage is its price, then your product does not have a sustainable competitive advantage.

Service industries are not spared from the terms dictated by an ever-more-demanding marketplace. Everything we have discussed relative to marketing and product follow-up applies to service providers, with some important exceptions. The biggest exception seems to be in the area of product costs. Here increases in prices of service to the final consumer often follow a path that is opposite that of product prices. This could be due to one factor or, more likely, a combination of factors, including government regulation, government deregulation, technological innovation, and the relative similarity of many service-related companies within a market sector.

For example, banking, an industry subject to all of the above factors, has been singularly successful in raising prices for the services banks provide. Today, in exchange for "free checking" (often accompanied by compensating balance requirements), we pay $30 to $35 dollars for an overdrawn check, $10 to $15 for electronic funds transfers ("Don't you love the term "convenience fee"?), and $5 to $8 for teller-assisted transactions. Additionally, in the face of accelerated and highly automated check-clearing practices, we are sometimes denied access for several days to funds deposited in our account. We point out these banking facts not to denigrate, but to congratulate. The transparency, similarity, and regulatory environments all have contributed to making it impossible for banks to gain a sustainable competitive price advantage, so prices for services play "follow the (ever-changing) leader." We chose banking as an example, but we observe the same scenario in service industries that fit this same profile, such as the enigmatic setting of airline fares.

Rarer, but not unheard of, is the marketing of services in a monopolistic or cartel-controlled environment. This happens most often in service industries at the regional or local level, thus escaping excessive regulatory scrutiny, but no less harmful economically than if it were to happen on a national scale. It will not be hard for the reader, after a little thought, to identify such industries operating at the local level.

Managing the marketing and managing the money may be the most important and visible management duties in today's corporate culture. More CEOs rise from these ranks than from any other corporate departments. Their success in these disciplines instills the confidence in others that they will be able to successfully deal with the concepts and problems faced by corporate chief executives. If you are identified as CEO, or COO material, you will likely be aware of this before you reach a senior management position. Be certain you want "it," because the dues are paid in advance. Just because you are not made aware of the conditions, perceptions, expectations, and relations does not mean they do not exist—they do. What you do know is what you have control over—results.

A record of excellent results, ethically achieved, is a résumé that needs no further embellishment. The marketing arena certainly serves as an attractive discipline in which to make your managerial mark. Big risk, big reward, no ambivalence goes unnoticed. This is the area where corporate expectations, unreasonable as they will inevitably become, are most evident and measurable, and that is probably just as it should be.

KEY 5

MANNERS

"Leadership rests not only upon ability, not
only upon capacity; having the capacity to lead is
not enough. The leader must be willing to use it.
His leadership is then based on truth and character.
There must be truth in the purpose and willpower
in the character."
—Vincent Lombardi

Think for a moment about all the ways your company and its culture are on public display on a daily basis. The public is aware of the products you produce, the building that you occupy, the people employed by the company, and the company's social interaction within the community. Users of your products or services will constantly judge the overall quality and value of your offerings. Neat and orderly physical facilities and appropriate social interactions will positively influence the general public. Those who interact with your employees on a business or social level will form opinions regarding your business by what they see and hear from your employees, true or false, for better or for worse.

Your corporate culture must continually foster and reinforce all the positives that make your company a good place to work and a good neighbor in the community. Positive company and trend images that took years to establish can be wiped out overnight by seemingly insignificant negatives that may manifest themselves with regard to your company, or even your industry, on the corporate landscape. For example, in a period of high energy prices, all providers are to blame, right? Your company likely did not precipitate the price increase, but you certainly share guilt by association. On an individual company basis, it seems that exceeding customers' expectations is the industry standard, and the tolerance for error is very small.

We all know of companies that are known for being "good places to work." There are actually rankings of good places to work published in business periodicals, based upon these companies' successfully meeting a set of criteria. While these companies are invariably successful in the marketplace with their products and services, it is their attention to the "people side" of the business that gets the attention and secures the top rankings. In fact, it could be argued that these companies' products and services are successful precisely because the human side of the business is handled so thoughtfully.

Does your business have the right policies in place, day in and day out, along with the right people to administer the policies, to make it a good place to work? Consistent application of the policies established is absolutely essential. Let's explore some ways to assure success.

Employee handbooks, properly prepared and presented, are effective resources for presenting the corporate culture, regarding employees, to newly hired personnel. Handbooks are not exhaustive in their scope and detail; rather, they present an overview of company policies with respect to company employees. Handbooks outline what the employees can expect from the company and what the company expects in return. Certain conformities and possibly behavior modifications are encouraged by a handbook's listing of unacceptable behavior, from excessive absenteeism and tardiness to drug use, theft, and insubordination, together with the disciplining action that would result from each type of infraction. Dress code, holidays, vacation policies, and a summary of available fringe benefits are usually included. Employees should be required to sign a form stating that they have read and understand the handbook, and pledge to return it should their employment terminate for any reason.

Every handbook has a tenor to its content. As this may be a new employee's first real contact with those for whom he or she will work, careful attention should be given to the style and presentation of the handbook's content. While some sections may call for a matter-of-fact presentation, other sections may need to include a statement that indicates where the employee may find additional information on the subject. This acknowledges that the company understands that the new employee may not know or understand the reasons for certain policies and that the company is anxious to help in that regard.

Some other handbook suggestions:

1. Eliminate jargon and buzzwords.
2. Include your mission statement.
3. Include a statement of your desire to make your company a "great place at which to work."
4. Include an appropriate equal opportunity statement.
5. Policies should be summarized, but behavior expectations should be clearly spelled out.

6. The presentation should be friendly, factual, and fair.
7. Reference should be made to the collective bargaining agreement in instances in which union policies are in effect.
8. Include an employment at will statement, if applicable. Because there are certain governmental restrictions on what you may or may not say in your handbook, you may want to have your first draft reviewed by an attorney schooled in labor law. Certain policies, such as the employment at will, should pass legal muster.

Common sense would seem to tell us that happy employees are more productive than are unhappy employees. This is undoubtedly true, albeit an oversimplification of all that a good employee needs in order to be "more productive." If happiness is indeed a key ingredient in the productivity recipe, it would make sense for managers to structure the corporate culture to aid in, rather than to impede, reaching this goal. In most instances, this goal is attainable without spending large sums on more elaborate break rooms, more fringe benefits, or longer breaks or vacations.

While the goal is attainable on a general scale, 100 percent employee participation in the contentedness is probably an unrealistic expectation. Why? Because people are people. Even well-educated, well-placed, well-paid people are going to have issues, and, if not dealt with, these issues can become a contagious disease in the workplace. When we talk about a corporate culture that incorporates good manners, we are talking about compassion, justice, and fairness in our human interactions on a daily basis.

If you practice good manners on an everyday basis in your interactions with every employee, your corporate culture will incorporate this attitude into the lifestyle of the workplace. While this may amount to behavior modification for some employees, think about just a few of the positives that can be realized just by treating your fellow workers with respect and a "do unto others" attitude:

- Good manners will result in more truthful, open communication among all employees.
- One possible "drawback" of working for your company is not simply eliminated; it is replaced by a huge positive.
- If good manners become pervasive, it is easier to recognize bad manners when they manifest themselves, as they inevitably will from time to time.
- New employees will learn from the start about appropriate behavior.
- No matter what your status within the organization, the most lasting legacy you leave will be the way you have treated others along the way.

It is a fact of corporate life that some people will lead and others will follow. Some will supervise; others will be supervised. Some will manage; others will be managed. Recall our reference to compassion, justice, and fairness. "Compassion" does not mean giving employees unlimited "chances," but it does mean trying to find a way to give them more than one. "Justice" means that the punishment or the reward must fit the crime or the achievement. "Fairness" means that compassion and justice must be evenly, equally administered. If only the application of these concepts were as easy as the definition. However, it is worth the effort.

If your company promotes from within, and managers generally come up "through the ranks," the corporate culture will have influenced and even modified their behavior through the years with regard to what we call "manners." Establishment of a culture of manners early in the company's life will be much easier to maintain than it will be to establish such a culture at a later date. The key is consistent application of good manners across the board. Human interaction in a corporate environment does not occur in a vacuum. It obviously has a direct effect on the participants, and it will be observed and judged by others. It is here that perception is as important as fact. The perception of compassionate justice being fairly applied is crucial.

The same holds true for rewards and awards. Fair application of the rules to determine the winner of a sales contest (which is almost always bad idea) will neutralize any argument. The ability to be fair on a consistent basis is a quality that every good supervisor or manager must possess. Favoritism will be detected, as will lack of compassion. Injustices will be detected, as will intolerance. Anything that occurs must be dealt with, especially if apologies are in order. One unresolved instance, allowed to pass, could destroy a career, a department, and possibly even a company.

Every manager should carry a second card in his or her wallet in addition to the little laminated mission statement card. The second card would simply read, "Do the Right Thing." By the way, if you don't have this section on manners up and running, skip the chapter on motivation—one doesn't work without the other.

Manners at the corporate level can be defined as being a good neighbor in the global business world. Some companies are handicapped at the outset on a local level, with necessarily noisy production facilities, a distribution system that taxes local roads and rails, and/or noxious or obnoxious fumes and particulates migrating from smoke stacks through the neighborhoods. These negatives are tolerated because the offensive factors tend to exist when and where jobs exist, and that is deemed an acceptable compromise. All businesses have obligations to the community in which they are located. The obligation is to operate the enterprise as ethically as possible and maintain a corporate culture that promotes social responsibility. Whether the business provides a product or a service or both, the obligation exists.

Ethical operation is of major importance because of the domino effect of unethical conduct. Major corporate scandals such as those which occurred at Enron and WorldCom were rife with unethical conduct, pervasive at the highest levels. The fallout was not confined to the wrongdoers. Innocent employees, major suppliers, and auditing firms were all impacted, as well as the communities in which the company had subsidiaries. The big companies make the news, but smaller instances occur every day with the same unfortunate results.

Unethical behavior, especially from a top company manager or official, cannot be tolerated. It is behavior that is inconsistent with company values and cannot be rationalized, marginalized, or justified. No mitigating circumstances can exist that would absolve unethical conduct, as it is not a recognized part of the corporate culture. It can and should be traced to individual acts, which must be dealt with.

Social responsibility is another aspect of corporate good manners, and one in which all employees should play a part. The successful company will be proud of its image in the local and global community, and that pride should be reflected in the physical aspects of the business. Interiors and exteriors should be neat, clean, and in good repair. The corporate culture should promote individual pride in the workplace: from the cubicle to the entire operation. It starts with managers who lead by example, it continues with corporate commitment of funds to improve and maintain the facilities, and it ends with each employee considering the maintenance of the workplace as "just a part of my job." Bean counters who whine about the "return on investment" for these types of expenditures need better eyeshades—it's there.

For those operating in a union environment, it should be pointed out that enforcing or renegotiating the terms of a collective bargaining agreement should offer no forums for setting aside manners and civility. While these issues can be and often are contentious, the entire process will be facilitated if the bargaining meetings and the accompanying public pronouncements are maintained at the highest levels. In the end, the quality and propriety of each side's position will be the single most influential factor in the negotiations. The debate over the proper role of labor unions in modern American business will continue for as long as people collectively gather to perform tasks that lead to a common goal.

Management's view is that "the union" does not adopt the goals for its members that management believes will lead to the success of the enterprise. Rather, union leadership fosters distrust among the rank and file with respect to management's motives, and in an effort to protect the members, leaders push for work rules that often seem to create needless production inefficiencies and bargain for wages and fringes, which, many observers claim, have resulted in the current flight to offshore production facilities where labor costs are much lower. Union leaders argue that the collective bargaining agreements currently in place are necessary for the protection of workers who would certainly suffer abuse in the absence of such contracts.

These are highly developed and often-conflicting philosophies, both of which contain elements of truth. Whether discussing the merits of a grievance or discussing the bargaining points of a new contract, all parties will benefit if their discussions are carried out in an atmosphere of civility and propriety appropriate to the seriousness of the situation.

For better or worse, today's corporate culture is more team-oriented than ever, and the question is no longer whether or not to utilize cubicles, but how many to utilize per given area of office space. Privacy in the workplace has, for many, become unattainable. Common workplace etiquette can do much to alleviate the stress and strain of day-to-day interaction with co-workers, managers, and supervisors. There is no one "right way" or "best way" to complete many tasks. No doubt most of us have workplace behaviors that may, to others, be irritating or distracting. We need to be as open as possible to feedback from others on workplace behavior or habits that do not, as our Constitution says, "promote the general welfare."

Planned social activities, such as holiday parties or picnics, may provide opportunities to get to know and possibly better understand those with whom we spend so much of our lives. In general, treat others as you would like to be treated, and do not allow issues you may have with other employees to go un-addressed. It can make all the difference.

Good manners tend to become invisible. They become the accepted operational norm and can quickly become something that is taken for granted. Let someone or some occurrence step outside of the established manners boundaries and it likely will be quickly detected due to its deviance from the established norms. This is a good thing. When the equilibrium can be restored on the side of manners, everyone wins.

MOTIVATION

"Unless a man believes in himself and makes a
total commitment to his career and puts everything
he has into it—his mind, his body, and his heart—what is
life worth to him? If I were a salesman, I would make
this commitment to my company, to the product,
and most of all, to myself."
—Vincent Lombardi

Jack had worked as a salesman for Worldwide Widgets for six years. For the last three years he had been the number one salesperson in terms of business booked, and in the past 12 months he had sold more of Worldwide's advanced widgets than the rest of the sales staff combined. Clearly, he was not the rising star; he was *the* star. One Monday Jack walked into the controller's office and presented an ultimatum: if there was not a $5,000 bonus included with Thursday's paycheck, then he would quit on Friday.

Tuesday morning, all of the initials (CEO, COO, and CFO) huddled in a hastily called strategy session. The meeting was as short as you might expect. Jack was, in corporate eyes, irreplaceable, as was the business he brought to the table. With vows of silence all around, it was agreed that the bonus would be paid with Thursday's paycheck. Friday, Jack's "Q-Day," came and went. Jack had received his bonus and all was well. Saturday morning, the overworked controller was met at the office by Jack, who handed over the keys to his company car along with his letter of resignation. "I didn't quit on Friday" was his only comment as he walked out of the stunned controller's office.

What can we learn from this story? Clearly, the salesman had arrived at a strategy which, by virtue of his "star" status with the company, had enriched him monetarily on his next to last day with Worldwide Widgets, and perhaps he believed he deserved the bonus, and perhaps he did deserve it. Did the suits make the wrong decision in giving it to him? Based on the information they had available to them at the time, yes. Where did they go wrong? It was in their interpretation of the data with which they had been presented. The forward-focus of the management team led them to believe that the bonus, although paid for past performance, would be a motivator for future success. Had the bonus been presented to Jack together with a continuing employment contract, the outcome may have been different.

The fact is that money, whether paid as an hourly wage, a salary, or a bonus, is seldom an effective motivational tool. Surveys among employees have consistently shown that employees do not rank financial incentives highest on their list of motivators. The closest corporate America comes to using money as an effective motivational tool is when it is used as a reward for specific performance—for achieving a specific goal as a company, team, or individual. For an item so far down the motivational pecking order, money gets a lot of attention in motivational studies. This high profile has led to the use of financial incentives in many cases when it is ineffective and can even harm a corporate motivational structure.

In a changing environment, the effectiveness of motivational tools at your disposal will vary in their application or their efficiency. As corporate culture evolves, change comes at a varying pace. As growth in employment occurs and employees wear fewer hats, change can be rapid and unpredictable, and oversight is critical. In fact, changes in employment and technology lead to the most accelerated changes in overall corporate culture. Adaptability and control become most important just at a time when uncertainty is most in evidence. Motivation becomes a key factor in improving, or even maintaining, group and individual performance.

If we preside over a company where employees need constant motivation, have we failed at our job of hiring the best available people for the jobs at hand? Is our corporate culture uninspiring? While it would be nice to have a group of coffee-fueled self-starting go-getters as employees, few if any companies would choose these adjectives to characterize their workers. People are not machines. People will work, and work hard, but their maintenance program must include motivation. You want your employees to be motivated, and you want to cultivate a corporate culture that fosters, or at least does not impede, employee motivation. As you develop this corporate structure, you need to ask a few key questions.

What do you want your employees to be motivated about? If you have done your job in the hiring process, you have in place individuals who will successfully and efficiently complete their jobs for the agreed-upon wage. Unless management has determined that every new and better idea will come from within management ranks, managers had better determine that, to be truly successful, often a company needs more from it employees than that they simply do their jobs. Company managers should want their employees to be motivated about their jobs, understand how their jobs fit into and contribute to the corporate vision, and understand how their jobs, performed efficiently, help to contribute to overall company success. (If your company has a published mission statement, it may be beneficial to integrate it into the corporate vision theme for continuity and focus.)

This means casting the "corporate vision" in an appealing way. Employees need to feel that the company is engaged in honorable, moral work, and has a corporate culture that responds to them as individuals while meeting the needs of society at an economic and social level. Less than honorable and ethical actions and intentions will quickly be discovered, and, suddenly, what people are motivated about is an ever-shifting goal that assures long-term disaster, as was seen in the WorldCom and Enron debacles. There, management's motivation to hit the numbers was not a goal that could readily be translated into a motivational tool to inspire the rank and file. Everyone is familiar with the results, with the greatest tragedy being the thousands of employees who were repaid for their productive efforts with devastating socioeconomic loss.

Once you have confidence that your corporate culture expresses your vision appealingly, truthfully, and successfully, the task becomes to determine how to best achieve an ongoing, motivational atmosphere while maintaining the underlying, but equally important, objectives of efficiency, profitability, and responsibility. Achieving this balance over time is truly the essence of management.

The menu of motivational items has changed and expanded in recent years as studies have become increasingly competent in measuring the effect of motivational elements on specific and overall performance. As our economy becomes more populated with and dominated by those involved in the service sector, specific performance has become harder to measure. Is Joe working more efficiently because he got a 10 percent raise, or because he got a newer, faster computer on which to perform his work? Unless you conclude that Joe dialed in a 10 percent efficiency increase in his personal work habits in response to the pay increase, you must conclude that it was primarily the technology that precipitated the increased output.

The following real-life exchange teaches us that, while the money was meant as a motivation, it was actually the new technology that did the job. Here are Joe's actual thoughts as this scenario unfolded.

Joe gets a raise:

"Hey, thanks for the raise. I deserved it."

Joe gets a new computer:

> "Hey, the job I am doing must be important. I have been entrusted with new technology. I like this new computer. Whether management knows it or not, it will make it easier for me to do my job. With this new machine I can be more productive and do a better job."

Whether the "new machine" is a computer or a punch press, it can be a motivational as well as a productive tool, so much so, that its motivational aspects should be factored into future measurement of that job's productivity and efficiency.

Other equally important motivational tools can and should be incorporated into the corporate culture by those charged with shaping it. Leadership needs to recognize that people are important. Let's remember that when we are talking about "human capital," we are talking about people, and as important as money and machines are, it is a company's people that, in the end, can make all the difference. The term "workers" has largely been replaced with such terms as "sales associates," "assistants," and "personnel" as the obfuscation of the English language continues in the face of political correctness. Whatever the term that we as a company choose, we are talking about the people who show up every day to do their job and are counting on you to give them the tools and the direction they need. A manager's challenge is: How can the corporate culture be shaped to include some of the most powerful motivational factors known to exist; and just what are those factors?

People, being different from each other, are motivated to different degrees by different factors. This being the case, should a manager spend a lot of time cultivating an atmosphere of (motivational) creativity at, say, an accounting firm? If the manager did, even if successful, he or she may not get the results intended. A wise approach may be to recognize that, as your company grows and jobs and departments become more specialized, they will be populated by supervisors and workers whose definition of successful performance at all levels will differ, sometimes in significant ways, from those of other departments in the same organization.

Motivational tools will differ in their effectiveness as well. Just as "creativity" should probably not be the motivational watchword at an accounting firm, a trip around the world might not be the best motivational award for, say, a company with a two-person sales staff. Will the award motivate your two-person sales staff over the life of the nine-month contest? The answer is probably yes. Will the negative effect on the losing salesperson's performance outweigh the positive effect of the contest? Will the long-term relationship of the sales staff with each other be irreparably harmed? The answers to the last two questions are probably both yes.

The answer here? Shorter contests, more discreet awards, clearly defined playing fields, a fair contest. Harder to administer? Maybe. More successful for you and your company? Yes. Your corporate culture should make it easy to motivate employees in a way that they can appreciate and understand, while at the same time reinforcing the corporate focus. A motivation/reward system should be management's equivalent way of saying "that's what I'm talking about!"

A cautionary word: If management gets good goal-oriented performance from its employees, but only in an environment where extended motivational factors are present, there is something wrong. When this situation is evident, it is time for serious corporate self-evaluation. Tough questions that demand honest answers. Just a few leading questions might be these:

- Are our shared corporate goals expressed, understood and realistic?
- Is our corporate culture too involved in motivational objectives: constant short-term goals that obscure the long-term goals of the company?
- Have we found it necessary to motivate people *not* to do things that negatively impact job performance? For example, have we established a negative reward system in which employees are rewarded for regular attendance, being on time, and adherence to break and to lunch times. In other words, do employees get rewarded for simply doing their jobs?
- Has our corporate culture, as it has evolved over the company's existence, become a tangled web of rules and regulations, conflicting, picky, and meaningless in the current environment?
- Do we have the right people for the job in each position, management included?
- Is our pay and benefit package fair and competitive for all?
- Do we provide a physical and emotional atmosphere in which employees want to work and in which they can achieve the goals expected of them in their particular jobs?

Asking and answering these and other similar questions will provide many insights into the motivational system that you have, perhaps inadvertently, established. The answers to some are easy. The answers to others will cascade into a whole series of questions that need to be answered.

In spite of what we have said about differing motivational factors between departments, there are some motivational techniques that seem to have virtually universal effectiveness, and (surprise!) they are usually the easiest, least costly methods available. All managers and supervisors should make sure that they have the following attributes:

1. A clean, consistent vision
2. Energetic leadership
3. Ethics above reproach

It is also important that their part in shaping the corporate culture includes ample use of the following:

1. Clear and realistic goal setting
2. Helpfulness
3. Support and cooperation
4. An open door
5. Willingness to change
6. Inclusiveness and empowerment—the "we" word
7. Talk "Team"—and walk the walk
8. Appreciation
9. Recognition for a job well done
10. Immediate correction of injustices
11. Willingness to give a second chance when appropriate—benefit of the doubt

You can think of other motivational attitudes as well. Motivation is the machine oil of the human element of a business. It can't be that "extra something." It must be an integral part of the way you conduct your business.

KEY 7

MENTORING

"They call it coaching but it is teaching. You do not
just tell them . . . you show them the reasons."
—Vincent Lombardi

One of the good things that has happened recently in American business is an increased focus on the values of mentoring. As these values have been probed and proven, mentoring has achieved more wide-ranging and formal recognition as a program to be incorporated into a company's corporate culture. However, mere mentioning of mentoring as a program is not enough. Like most good business programs, a good mentoring program does not just happen but requires input and recognition from all levels of the organization. Implementation of mentoring programs may in fact require several of our new-scope meetings.

Mentoring in our context does not include the crash-course training program normally undertaken by a staff employee to train his or her replacement employee during the two-week notice period. It is, rather, a program with a long-term focus, designed to encourage specific job performance and based on interpersonal relationships within the business environment. There are definite characteristics of well-targeted mentoring programs that are general in nature, not confined to a specific mentoring relationship.

These top programs include the following characteristics:

Interpersonal relationships play a crucial role. Most often there is a one-to-one relationship. In certain circumstances, a program may start with a two-to-one or even a three-to-one mix, but after an exclusionary process, a one-to-one set seems to work best. The one-to-one relationship is that of a subordinate (subject) being mentored by a superior (mentor).

The mentoring process is highly unique to the individuals involved. The corporate culture that supports the mentoring process will, of course, be a more familiar operating environment for the mentor. To what extent behavior modification is required of the subject in order for him or her to effectively operate within the corporate culture will become readily apparent at the outset of the process. The fact that this may be necessary—to some greater or lesser extent—shows the uniqueness of the process. No two processes are going to be identical in structure, content, or duration—even when the desired outcomes are identical.

The fact that one process takes longer or is quicker than another should not be a basis for inferring anything about the quality of the mentor, the subject, or the outcome. It is not a race but is in fact a process whose end would be very difficult to determine. A mentor-subject relationship is usually long term, lasting until one or both of the participants relocate or shift their corporate focus. It is not unusual for the mentoring relationship to develop into a lifelong friendship between the participants.

The object of a mentoring relationship is, through the mentoring process, to preserve a specific operating practice that has proven to be effective in the past in its positive effect on corporate performance. Thus, there may be mentoring programs in virtually every department of the organization. The process does involve a teaching-learning relationship. The teaching is not usually task-specific but is a passing on of the "why," with less emphasis on the "how." There are corporate disciplines that do not lend themselves to the mentoring process. For example, an accountant does not need to learn accounting (the "how") or be convinced of its benefit to the company (the "why"). Thus, the accounting departments of most businesses probably do not have a very strong mentoring program until the controller or CFO positions are impacted.

It is important for managers and supervisors to present their thoughts and direct their efforts in a unified way, achieving continuity of thought and direction regardless of who is directing the action. This type of leadership calls for a strong mentoring program that instills the values and morals of the corporate culture into the subject's everyday actions and decisions. Companies with well-thought-out philosophies of the various aspects of their corporate culture will have little trouble getting subjects to "buy in" to the business philosophy being presented. Highly detailed standard operating procedure manuals and job descriptions are all well and good, but it is the unwritten "why" that makes it all work. Mentoring occurs in virtually every organization, but it is more effective when it is a recognized program in every department in which it exists.

The typical one-on-one relationship has a usually unspoken component that colors the process. The subject is being mentored so that he or she may later replace the mentor. Some mentors are nearing retirement, while others are climbing the corporate ladder and may themselves be subjects in another mentoring relationship. If an individual is to be mentored as part of a formal mentoring program, it will not be a secret to him or her or to others within the organization. In most cases the subject will be—or should be—pleased and excited to be the focus of such a program. In all probability, the subject has demonstrated both a willingness and an ability to do most or all of the following that help to assure the success of a mentoring relationship:

- Work hard
- Learn new jobs, and new ways of doing current jobs
- Modify behavior when necessary to conform to corporate cultural norms
- Perform the mentor's duties

As the subject, you also have responsibilities which, if fulfilled, will help to assure the success of the process:

- To come to the process with an open mind. To accept the "ground rules" as expressed and to respect the relative status of the mentor as it relates to the organization
- To treat the process as an opportunity rather than a burden or an additional duty. You are being evaluated on your outlook as well as your output.
- To ask for help or clarification when necessary
- To accept criticism or praise for what is said, not necessarily for how it is said. Some of the best and brightest business leaders are remarkably inept when it comes to criticizing or praising co-workers.
- Not to set a deadline for yourself. This is a long-term process which you do not control.

The subject must approach the mentoring process with no preconceived notions that he or she has been "selected" or is being "fast tracked," even if it is accurate to say so. Those who are selected can be unselected, and the blindness of ego can derail that fast-track career. If this unfortunate circumstance occurs, it is highly unlikely that the chance for this type of program at this particular firm will be offered again.

As a mentor, your primary responsibilities in a mentoring relationship are to do the following:

- Accurately—and even passionately—impart to the subject the vital chapters of the unwritten "why" in the job description manual
- Make sure that the subject understands the nature and the purpose of the relationship. You control the process: what information will be shared, how it will be shared, and when. An expectant rather than a surprised subject will be more receptive to the information to be shared in the process
- Observe the subject with an eye toward ultimate success of the process. You cannot be consumed by the day-to-day minutiae of the relationship.
- Provide helpful, constructive feedback on the subject's progress. Give constructive criticism and praise, both where necessary.
- Be ready and willing to learn yourself. The mentoring process can be a mind-expanding exercise for all concerned.

Look for the mentoring process to become more popular within successful business organizations. If you are in a position to become a mentor, keep a supply of 3 x 5 note cards handy to make written notes of important points that need to be made to your subject at the appropriate time. However desirous it may be to pass along corporate culture and job procedures to shorten the learning curve and assure continuity, the process will fail without formal recognition of the program and an active, goal-oriented mentor-subject relationship. Recognition of the relationship gives the subject and the mentor the necessary focus on the process and establishes equally necessary accountability for the outcome of the program.

KEY 8

MEETINGS

"Individual commitment to a group
effort—that is what makes a team work,
a company work, a society work, a
civilization work."
—Vincent Lombardi

Charlie is the CEO of a mid-size manufacturing company. As with most well-run companies, Charlie's business has an open-door policy and is a company that fosters and encourages employees' involvement and empowerment. Charlie's office has no other chairs or couches besides his desk chair. None of the members of Charlie's senior staff have seating other than their own chair in their offices. There is a relatively small conference room in a windowless corner adjacent to the boiler room. It is equipped with a nice table and seating for up to 10 in straight-backed wooden chairs.

Up until two years ago, this Spartan landscape was not the case in Charlie's office, and comfortable seating was in abundance for everyone who wished a seat for "a meeting." Charlie instituted the change when he was elected CEO by the company's board of directors, moving from his position as senior vice president. Charlie had long believed that the company had missed valuable opportunities and was operationally handicapped by the need to seek and acquire a consensus decision on virtually every change enacted at the corporate level. Senior managers were abdicating their decision-making and policy-implementing power to management-by-committee via meetings, and the resultant bureaucracy caused policy changes to be enacted with glacial speed, with uncertain accountability, and with inconsistent follow-up.

Charlie thought that changing the environment might help speed up decisions. His company managers now have stand-up meetings in their offices, conferences in the hallways, and committee meetings in an agenda-accelerating, cramped, uncomfortable conference room. Charlie found out that he was right in his assumption: the changes in reaction times, new policy implementation rates, and performance monitoring have been jaw dropping. All employees doing their jobs and assuming responsibility for decisions and activities within their spheres of authority has eliminated most meetings entirely and has reduced the required attendance for and duration of meetings for the few that do need to be held.

This may seem to be an extreme reaction to a situation that some may not even consider being a problem (but it is a true story). While it may be unfair to take a broad-brush approach to meetings by saying that they are unnecessary, it is undoubtedly true that a majority of meetings at most enterprises could be eliminated or reduced to a quick exchange of ideas. Considering just the economic cost of having a meeting should give one pause. Salaries of attendees before (planning and research), during (actual meeting time), and after (follow-up, implementation, etc.) a meeting will be significant cost items. Other cost items quickly add up for supplies, help with ancillary tasks, and, of course, coffee.

Have we created a corporate culture that encourages meetings? Do we exist in an agenda-driven society that has extended its reach into the corporate offices of America? What types of actions or intentions should require a meeting? When every decision is made by a group or a committee, or as a result of a meeting, are we acknowledging that our corporate culture lacks an empowerment initiative? When to have or not have a meeting is a question that may not be easily answered, but relatively specific guidelines should be proposed to help. The economic and opportunity cost of too many meetings is too great to ignore. Therefore, tough questions need to be asked and answered. Here are a couple:

1. Can we make this decision without a meeting? To answer this question, you must have a firm grasp of the decision being required. In many cases, thinking this through will allow you to reach a conclusion about the problem and the (now abated) need for a meeting.

2. Does our corporate culture truly empower managers to make decisions and implement policies as a result? How far does empowerment extend? Here, corporate practice often trumps unspoken but generally understood policies and verbal policies. If employees are "totally empowered" to make policy decisions within their departments but the ramifications of less-than-perfect decisions or implementation is that the employee is shown the door, then you have a meeting-driven organization in which change comes by committee.

This mind-set filters down to the lowest levels of the organization when the buyers of office supplies are meeting to decide whether to buy legal pads by the case or continue to buy them by the package. True empowerment means, among other things, that you understand your sphere of influence and authority within the company, you make reasoned, informed decisions, and you take responsibility for the results of those decisions. Fair and balanced treatment is so important to motivation and empowerment. Literally years of corporate culture development in these two vital areas can be wiped out overnight by situations that employees perceive as inequitable or unjust treatment. Employees who are encouraged to use their empowerment to move the company forward must believe that other managers "have their back" and that company officers up to the CEO are going to give properly structured initiatives the benefit of the doubt.

When there are too many meetings in a company that did not have them before, there is a problem that needs to be addressed. Enough employees to do the work and employees who understand their work and are allowed to do it are the backbone of a successful organization. There is a saying "if you are meeting weekly, you are meeting weakly," which is not far off the mark. Hire the right people, instill your values, philosophy, and goals, and let them do their job. Allow for failures and reward success. Encourage empowerment.

CEOs should be provided with a detailed agenda of every proposed meeting, and the agenda should include a list of those expected to attend. The CEO should also receive a summary report after every meeting. This requirement alerts meeting moguls to the fact that the CEO of the company considers the frequency and the agenda of meetings to be important enough for him or her to be kept personally informed about each and every one. This requirement has a wondrous effect.

There are, or course, occasions when meetings must be held. When decisions or change in a department will affect those in another or when major initiatives are under consideration, then the opinions of others are often required. In these cases, someone must run the meeting. If it is you, here are a few suggestions to make it a good meeting:

1. Develop a detailed, purpose-driven agenda and distribute it far enough in advance to give everyone a chance to arrange his or her schedule. Explain clearly and concisely the problem(s) to be discussed.
2. Give thought to attendees. Do you need input from a valued customer or from someone in the clerical or production department?
3. Give the meeting a start time and an end time.
4. Start the meeting at the announced time. End the meeting at the announced time.
5. Use a whiteboard, overhead projector, or pad and easel to highlight major points.

6. Appoint someone to prepare a meeting summary, including, if appropriate, a list of action items to be researched or accomplished. If it is apparent that action items need to be addressed in order to reach a decision, make those the focus of this meeting, because you will need another one to share and interpret the data collected.

7. If you sense a consensus, try to draw it out.

8. Keep the focus. If the meeting is one of a series, make sure everyone has done his or her homework prior to the meeting. Expect it. Don't give anyone a pass.

9. If a series of meetings, such as strategic planning sessions, are being scheduled, consider holding the meetings off-site and with the services of a facilitator—someone who is a consultant or who has been through the process before. Both of these options should save time by eliminating distractions and should improve the quality of the sessions.

10. Take advantage of technology in meeting planning and execution. Instant messaging, speakerphones, picture phones, and other technological conveniences offer real opportunities to increase efficiency, decrease costs by reducing travel, and increase productivity by allowing multitasking during the session.

You may need to adjust your corporate culture as it applies to meetings. Meetings certainly have a place, but if there are too many or they do not produce the desired results, they can also be warning signs. The need to respond and adapt in today's global economy is greater than ever. No meeting ever greased the wheels of change.

Note: You may need to have a meeting to discuss whether or not to have fewer meetings!

MOBILITY

"Winning is not
everything—
but making
the effort
to win
is."
—Vincent Lombardi

It is inevitable that as a company grows, it will become necessary to add employees to the workforce. Over time, as this growth continues, it is also inevitable that a company will experience "bureaucratic creep." This is a slow but significant occurrence as the corporate culture evolves and, in spite of the negative connotation of the term we have used to describe the effect, it does not necessarily have to be a negative for the company. Since the growth of corporate bureaucracy is indeed inevitable, it can and must be managed to minimize negative effects that may evolve. Along the road, there is the constant temptation to compare one's corporate operation to others', regionally or nationally. The most visible manifestation of this practice is product comparison—benchmarking.

In reality, corporate comparisons are inevitable and pervasive, and, for the most part, have a positive impact on business operations. When you observe a group of CEOs having lunch at the club, or a group of IT guys at the diner having coffee, it is likely they are talking shop, and it is also likely that all will benefit from the exchange of information. No one company has a corner on effective management practices. Effectively decreasing bureaucracy and increasing mobility is the key to your ability to take full advantage of "operational opportunities" that are inevitably discovered along the way as growth and bureaucratic creep begin to take hold.

Mobility implies the ability—not the need—to change, and that difference can make all the difference. A few companies are kept small by design. Managers all have open doors, most wear several hats, and management style is an efficient combination of managing by walking around and managing for results. As companies who chose to do so get larger and more diverse, the management practices become more segmented, and managers wear fewer hats, close their doors, and manage by respect (real or perceived). We are not disparaging the growth cycle of corporations; that's just the way it is.

It is somewhat ironic that the global players are almost required to be ponderous, dealing on a multinational level with a myriad of regulations, tax laws, product regulations, and geographically instituted restrictions, while at the same time are likely the ones most to benefit from the responsiveness to change that can be achieved by making mobility a necessary component of each bureaucratic initiative. As organizations grow, managers are often victims of the intellectually vapid, yet true cliché that says they "can't see the forest for the trees." If you have policies or procedures in place that are there because that's the way it has always been done, then those policies and procedures need to be examined or re-examined. There should be good, solid reasons why "things" are structured as they are, and everyone should be aware of why those reasons exist. Mobility should be an uncompromised component of every manager's set of goals and objectives.

If there is a company or companies out there that you admire for their successful ability to efficiently incorporate change into their organizations (the adjective *successful* and adverb *efficiently* are there for an important reason), there are several important questions you need to ask before undertaking a more enthusiastic comparison:

1) Why do I like what I see?
2) Are my perceptions accurate?
3) How would my company benefit from changes being considered—in the long run? In the short run?
4) Is the cost/benefit ratio obviously positive?
5) Would our corporate culture be accepting of the changes required to achieve this responsiveness?

Always remember that you are comparing apples to oranges. As we have said before, no two companies are even close to being identical.

Maintaining mobility, like maintaining a garden, requires constant vigilance to keep the weeds out. Company loyalty is great, but "we're the best" attitudes can be exclusionary to a fault. *Compromise, change, what if,* and *why* should all be words that are common to your corporate culture. One of the more successful aspects of strategic planning sessions can be to bring in individuals with knowledge of business—but not your business—and to explore with them the ramifications of going on a bureaucratic diet, and how to get your employees to buy in to the program.

Is mobility always a good thing? Remember, mobility implies the *ability* to change, not the necessity. If that is a referential definition, then the answer is almost certainly yes. Sometimes, events occur or circumstances change in ways that present so many immediate challenges to corporate mobility that alarm bells go off in the minds of even the most isolated of corporate managers. Please allow a personal occurrence to serve as an example.

Years ago, I was working for a manufacturer of industrial products. A French manufacturing conglomerate acquired the company. Here is a summary of the immediate situation: instant geographical and cultural disparities, unfamiliar products introduced to unfamiliar markets with unfamiliar regulations. Senior management was replaced with or augmented by executives from the French parent. (The welcome dinner was, awkwardly, consumed in almost total silence due to the language barrier.) Due diligence? Cost savings by eliminating duplicate expenditures? Product standardization initiatives? What could have been an exciting time became anxiety time. Suddenly every task seemed insurmountable, and *mobility* as a watchword had been replaced by that old standby—*survival.*

A company is mobile when its people and its culture are open to change, anticipate change, constructively critique change, and actually incorporate change when it will result in improved future performance. A company concerned with maintaining this ability to respond will also plan for change prior to the need or an event triggers the need for a change. Succession planning, contingency planning, disaster planning, mergers and acquisitions planning, growth planning. These types of exercises, as well as normal departmental planning, should all incorporate the need to be flexible, mobile, proactive, and effectively reactive to any situation that may occur. When natural or man-made disasters or unlikely events befall a company, the manager's ability to steer the ship through the storm will be judged by those on the outside looking in. Second-guessing will be the order of the day, and what you could have or should have done had better be just what you did.

Many times a company's reputation and its resultant success will depend, to a greater or lesser extent, on how well it performs under the pressure of unexpected events. Your job should be to make sure that unexpected events are not unanticipated events in your planning processes. Plan your work; work your plan.

Mobility does not only mean the ability to quickly and efficiently respond to change in the business environment; it also means having the ability to lead the way, to adjust business practices proactively as business conditions warrant. A corporate culture that "builds in" mobility will be well positioned to respond to change, while minimizing the chance of catastrophic consequences.

The need for optimizing corporate mobility is greater today than at any other time in history. The factors that make this statement true are the existence today of realities such as competition on a truly global scale, instantaneous communication and transfer of information, tremendous technological change, demands for increased business transparency, and the seemingly pervasive atmosphere of political and cultural unrest in which we must function. Given this set of circumstances, would anyone be surprised to learn of the creation and staffing of a position known as "corporate mobility manager"?

Add to these dynamics the increasing pressure of government intervention and the dichotomies precipitated by differing political ideologies, and one can see that maintaining mobility may require the awareness, analysis and management of events and conditions beyond the company's direct control. The burden of government regulation is not evenly distributed, and a large multi-national firm can be subject to a dizzying, sometimes conflicting set of international regulations. The net effect of regulatory compliance is often in conflict with the concept of maintaining mobility.

Plan for mobility. Reactive and proactive mobility are indispensable components present in every successful business. Competitive advantages are most often the result of careful planning, and a mobile, "nimble" company has a built-in advantage over their competitors as a result of incorporating mobility into their corporate culture.

MERGERS

"Leaders are made, they are not born. They are made by hard
effort, which is the price which all of us must pay to
achieve any goal that is worthwhile."
—Vincent Lombardi

It seems strange that mergers so often seem to occur on an industry-specific basis. For example, for a period of time, the drug industry may undergo a round of mergers, acquisitions, or consolidations, which eventually end, only to be followed by a round of activity in the broadcasting or banking industry, and so on. (Mergers and acquisitions are, in fact, different from each other, but similar enough in their inception and execution to be considered together without significant distortion of the processes.) The reasons for industry-wide activity may or may not be known, understood, or valid (maybe the CEOs just think "Hey, that's a good idea; let's do that!"), but there are usually one or more specific reasons for undertaking a merger or acquisition, such as the following scenarios:

- A company has expressed a desire to participate in a merger, or to be acquired, or to divest itself of a specific division.
- A company has adopted a growth strategy that includes merger or acquisition, or already has a history of growth through these methods.
- Two (or more) companies agree that their combined operations could be organized so as to increase market share, lower operating expenses, act as a barrier to others contemplating entry into the marketplace, improve R&D operations, or provide other efficiencies that would be desirable going forward.
- The hostile takeover of another company is seen as desirable for any one or more economic or market-driven reasons, such as access to otherwise unavailable technology, seemingly impenetrable market sectors, or specifically desirable management expertise resident at the target company.

- Industry-wide consolidations all seem to make sense when they occur in response to factors such as newly emerging technology, new or revised government regulations, deregulations, or tax law revisions.

These are but a few of the reasons for merger and acquisition activity. Depending, usually, upon the relative size and willingness of the target company to the proposed action, a merger or acquisition will rate a paragraph, a column, or a headline in the *Wall Street Journal*. In human terms, however, the effect of a merger or acquisition can have a significant toll on the merging operations and morale of the companies involved. If the disparity in size is great, the target company will disappear in the marketplace, quickly absorbed by the acquiring conglomerate. The human toll can be daunting, as entire departments such as accounting and marketing are eradicated, and R&D projects and dollars are redirected, reorganized, expanded, or abandoned.

The result of such activity may seem to outsiders as disorganized, ruthless, and counterproductive, and indeed, the stock price of the acquiring company may reflect the public's (or at least the stockholders') belief that efficiencies to be gained do not warrant the action or may, in fact, have an adverse effect on overall corporate function.

Hopefully, prior to and behind the scenes, much due diligence has taken place. In the due diligence process, areas of potential cost savings are identified and quantified, as are market share issues. Where common customers or common products exist, care must be taken to assure that a combination is really for the best. Intangible aspects, such as public perception and market acceptance of the merger, must also be considered.

Finally, the combination must pass regulatory muster with agencies such as the Federal Trade Commission and often with foreign regulatory agencies as well. These groups may impose limitations on combined operations or require divestiture or spin-offs of some related operations prior to approving the final agreement. In many cases, certain regulatory agencies may have a great deal to say about the capacities and abilities of the resultant combined entity, especially in areas such as the airline, broadcast, and utility industries.

Are most mergers and acquisitions successful? Often the answer is a qualified yes or no, and it depends upon whom you ask and what may be your acceptable definition of success. If you have the chance to participate in a merger/acquisition exercise, take advantage of the opportunities inherent in the process for a business education unlike anything you have ever experienced.

After a period of time has passed, merged companies that produce and sell commodity products at the retail level my find that their brand identity is as strong or stronger than ever. This may be due to the effectiveness of advertising and marketing efforts of the company at the individual product level. Conglomerates that are a melting pot of mergers and acquisitions may do very well at meeting their corporate objectives, but this is almost always due to the successful marketing of their individual products or services. Conglomerates do not market themselves as conglomerates, but rather as individual products. You don't often see advertising for General Mills, Proctor and Gamble, or YUM Brands but you do for the products they bring to the market. Each of these companies, as well as many others, is or has been a player in the mergers and acquisitions market and each spends a considerable amount in media marketing campaigns. You don't get a discount coupon for YUM Brands, but you may for KFC or Taco Bell or Pizza Hut, which are all members of the YUM group. Mergers and acquisitions can be exciting and stressful, and doing it right often means doing it the "hard way", but the rewards of successfully acquiring and integrating another entity (or of being acquired and integrated) can be tremendous and a source of accomplishment for all involved.

Other business combinations exist in addition to mergers and acquisitions. Occasionally, a business (i.e., the managers of a business) may reasonably conclude that another existing business, which may or may not be a competitor and may or may not be of similar or equal size in terms of sales, market share, employees, or other measurement values, has a business practice, product, or market niche that would be beneficial to the interested company. Additionally, they may conclude that they have something to bring to the table which, when combined with the other business, may make both stronger in one or more ways. Sometimes, these conclusions are reached through benchmarking exercises, or they may reveal themselves through discussions with common customers, vendors, or employees of other companies that are aware of each company's strengths, weaknesses, and capabilities.

When these circumstances present themselves, it is often in the best interest of both companies (or more) to explore the opportunities that may exist if certain strengths of each company were brought to bear on opportunity areas common to all involved companies—not a merger or acquisition, but more of a joint venture, which could be market—or product-specific, time-period-limited, or goal-specific. Joint ventures are attractive for their relative simplicity, their avoidance of many regulatory obstacles, their possibly limited duration, the preservation of each company's identity, and their limited impact on the human capital dimension of each company's operations.

On the other hand, they may be unattractive because, once made public, the ventures expose vulnerabilities the participating entities are seeking to overcome by combining, and which can be exploited if the joint venture is unsuccessful in achieving its goal or goals.

Companies involved in strategic planning or growth scenario planning often come to the realization that strategically important functions required to achieve their stated goals need to be augmented or strengthened to perform to expectations. Acquiring the necessary efficiencies through a joint venture may be a more expeditious and less costly way to achieve the desired results.

This partnership should be entered into only after there is a clear and mutually agreeable understanding of the goals to be achieved, the methods to be employed by each in achieving the goals, the interim objectives to be met, the anticipated timeline, and the ongoing responsibility and accountability to be assumed by each member of the group. Previously captive resources of each member company will now be devoted to achieving the goals of the joint venture, and much of the business practices of each participant will be exposed to the astute observer.

Mutual trust and cooperation will be valuable assets to share during the term of the joint venture. Clearly defined goals and objectives are also necessary components of an ongoing, successful venture. If you are a participant in the management of a company that is considering a joint venture, consider other possible alternatives to a joint venture in achieving the goals that have been developed.

For example, if your goal is to increase market penetration and thus market share, what needs to be done to achieve this goal? If you decide that, say, strengthening your brand identity is the key, this may be achievable by utilizing a consultant or market research team rather than establishing a joint venture.

Of course, if you are right and market share increases, a joint venture may be the way to quickly increase production and back-office operations by adding already-existing productive capacity and related functions that could be provided by a willing, responsive, and currently underutilized partner.

Many joint ventures perform very well and go on to do many projects together and to accomplish more than either company could if each operated independently. Those that fail often do so quickly, with the primary reason being confusion resulting from unclear goals and poorly defined expectations with regard to each company's performance. In mergers and acquisitions and in joint ventures, the planning, goals, expectations, timing, and execution are all keys to success. There are probably no other corporate activities that offer such potential for huge successes or huge disasters, all on public display.

Your planning should reflect the realization that anything could happen and there will undoubtedly be unforeseen circumstances that must be dealt with. Planning your work and then working your plan is a saying that was never more important than in the business of mergers, acquisitions, and joint ventures.

MISSTEPS

"In great attempts, it is
glorious even to fail."
—Vincent Lombardi

It seems that, almost weekly, readers of the *Wall Street Journal, Investors Business Daily,* and other business-related publications are able to read about a company that is in the spotlight for what we will call, for want of a better all-encompassing term, a "misstep." A misstep can be an accidental event that brings with it some type of misfortune. A misstep can be an event beyond the control of the affected business or industry that causes an unfortunate result. A misstep can also be an intentional act that harms a company, its employees, its future, its reputation, or its very existence. In a dynamic business environment, operating in a free market economy and largely free from government intervention and regulation, missteps can and do occur, and when they do, the effects can become the subject of newspaper and magazine articles, the nightly national news, and even Leno and Letterman jokes.

Under the "protection" of government control, the results of many missteps are not made public, or are at least controlled as to what information is released. How much do we really know about the nuclear event in Chernobyl or the gas leak in Bhopal, India? Scientists and engineers will tell you we don't know enough; Russia and India say we know all we are going to know.

In our society almost the opposite is true. Although the phrase "the public's right to know" is not to be found in our Constitution or The Bill of Rights, it has come to mean that we believe we are entitled to as much information as we would like about whatever we would like. If information is not forthcoming, a legion of reporters armed with Freedom of Information documents will make sure that disclosure is complete to their satisfaction. What interests us about a misstep is not necessarily what we need to know about the event. The identity of those involved is not necessarily a "need to know" item, but if the misstep occurs in the form of corporate fraud or dishonesty, an introspective manager may learn valuable lessons applicable to his or her position and the company by learning about the motives, opportunity, and MO of the individuals involved. Learn all you can about the facts surrounding any misstep, whether accidental, intentional, or circumstantial, and then sort out the useful information as it may apply to your situation.

A businessman will tell you that the proper response to a misstep involves the implementation of a contingency plan—as if it were like flipping a switch. The truth is that contingency plans are, together with succession plans, the most often overlooked business plans. Besides, who can put together a plan for each and every contingency that may occur? You can't, but these are general principles that can and should be discussed for possible implementation should a misstep occur in which others may take an interest:

- Who is the public voice of the company? One person should be designated as the company spokesperson in instances in which public pronouncements may be necessary. It might be wise for the designated individual to carry a "spokesperson" or "public relations" title. It would also be wise for this person to be familiar with media relations and even with the individuals with whom he or she may have occasion to speak. Larger companies routinely hire individuals with a media background to speak on their behalf. Public speaking should not be an issue with these spokespersons. Courses in public speaking and media-type dialogue and discussion are available and should be utilized if there is any question about this issue. An inadvertent misstatement, a nervous laugh, an omitted phrase—any or all can be seized upon and become the focal point instead of the incident under discussion. All employees should be made aware of the spokesperson's existence, identity, and purpose so that they may direct all inquires, politely, in the right direction.
- Attitudes and pronouncements should be as positive as possible, while being absolutely truthful in content.
- If you were doing it correctly before the incident, it should be business as usual as much as possible after. If you were due for a change, this *might* be the time to make it.
- Otherwise unconnected plans or events, even if previously planned, will be connected by others to missteps by virtue of "time and space." Consider the status quo as preferable to optional changes during the period of time when incidents are being discussed and investigated. People get a lot of exercise jumping to conclusions, and smart companies will assess the impact of

appearances as well as facts. These can be times when meetings *are* called for. There is one game that everyone can and will play. It is that of being a "Monday morning quarterback." After the fact, even the most remote consequences seem obvious, should they occur. Remembering that being defensive is offensive, and therefore tempered responses are the order of the day.

- While it may be possible to make a molehill out of a mountain, or to make lemonade from the lemons, these propitious outcomes should not be sought at the expense of corporate ethics, accountability, morality, and honesty, any of which, if damaged or called into question, could take years, if ever, to repair.

In the case of missteps—incidents or accidents—that are not on the public radar, all of the above generalized contingencies and guidelines should be part of any plan implemented to address any situation. The company's concern should be to properly and adequately address the situation as efficiently as possible. Keep in mind that someone more important than the public is watching, waiting, and forming opinions: your employees. Years of hard work can evaporate overnight if the perceptions of a resolution are that the outcome was unjust or did not address the (real) problem, or that the situation was ineptly managed. Aggressive honest management of the situation, with accountability and responsibility for the consequences, is the only proper way to address a misstep, be it internally contained or "out there" for all the world to see.

One thing that cannot be overlooked by those involved or by those observing and learning is the end result of the incident. You have probably adequately followed through if you can, to your satisfaction, answer these questions:

- Could this happen to us? Why? Why not?
- If it did happen, what happened?
- How did it happen?
- What was the timeline from beginning to end?
- What changes did the company implement to prevent a recurrence of the incident (assuming the company survived)?
- What changes, if any, should we implement to prevent a recurrence?
- Would we survive a similar occurrence? Why? How?
- What do I think the company's response should have been?
- What do I think our company should do now? Why?

It is conceivable, though not probable, that you could become involved in a corporate misstep of "Enronian" (i.e. brobdingnagian) proportion. In instances such as this, the facts and circumstances would be such that most reasonable individuals would conclude that the continued existence of the company as a going concern will not be possible. At such a time, the human drama begins, as jobs, careers, and earned pensions evaporate and human capital becomes human casualties. There is a time to find and punish the guilty, but this is not it. Management, compassion, and empathy may be hard when you are among the affected, but this is a time when compassionate management is appropriate and appreciated. More often, missteps are "simply" tough times, best handled by tough people.

KEY 12

MOVING ON

"Some of us will do our jobs well
and some will not, but we will
all be judged by only one thing—
the result."
—Vincent Lombardi

Throughout this book we have discussed some of the ways in which today's businesses differ from those of our fathers, and their fathers. There is a significant difference that occurs on a personal level that should not be overlooked. Please allow a personal story to illustrate my forthcoming point:

My father served in World War II, and at the end of the war, he returned home, secured a job in a field in which he had interest and ability, and worked there until his retirement more than 30 years later. This is a familiar, unremarkable scenario for many of those who comprise the workforce in what Tom Brokaw has called "The Greatest Generation."

To generations "X" and "Y," this story seems strange and unfamiliar. Today's career-bound generation will change jobs and geographically relocate between three and seven times, on average, before they find their career niche. Why is this so? There are probably several reasons, one of which could be the attraction of a job that did not even exist several years earlier. We are so different from the "Greatest Generation" that there really can be no apples-to-apples comparison. It is simply a fact that a vast majority of us will find ourselves, for one reason or another, "moving on."

We are a nation of 300 million people. Unless you are a child, chances are that you are now or have in the past been a member of America's "working class". At any given time there are, on average, between 4% to 6% of workers who are unemployed, which means, to the government at least, that these individuals are currently looking for work but are unable to find gainful employment, for whatever reason. As those of my generation (the post World War II baby-boomers) now are beginning to retire, the retired segment of our society has begun to grow as a percentage of the total population. Within the employed population there are a number of sub-groups that have been identified and labeled by our classification—obsessed society. We have government and civilian employees. We have the workers who work because they want to and those who work because they have to. We have the under-employed and the over-employed. We have management and rank-and-file. People move into and out of these groups for reasons too numerous to mention. We are going to take a closer look at three of the realities that individuals may encounter in moving out of the ranks of the employed, if only for a short time, and the personal consequences that may be involved in each.

Reason 1: Termination

If you are performing your job well, it is usually because you enjoy your job and have the requisite ability. The perfect job combines your avocation with your vocation. (That would equate to me playing golf for a living.) Few of us attain this goal, but that does not mean it should not be a goal. (I am distressed when I hear parents and teachers constantly point out to children the odds of attaining a career in professional sports. We need to encourage big dreams in sports as well as in science.)

Termination is tough when it happens, and usually, but not always, is looked back upon as for the best. Termination usually occurs for a reason. There are a few characteristics common to most termination profiles: a relatively short time on the job, poor job performance, and lack of interest and advancement potential in the eyes of your supervisor. Moving on via termination under these circumstances is almost always viewed as "for the best" after the passage of time.

The major negative factors include the stigma attached to your résumé, not leaving on your own terms, and the possibility that you will be released into a less-than-desirable job market. Most people are hired in part for their potential as well as for the job they initially acquire. If the potential is not there, it is best to cut the ties and move on.

In management positions, job performance alone is not usually enough to carry the day. It's not only results, it's how you get them, and whether your business practices reflect the corporate values and the existing corporate culture. Terminations are not easy for either party. If you find yourself packing up your belongings and being escorted to the door, use the pain as educational motivation. Be hard on yourself, fix what went wrong, and move on and move up.

Subsequent to a termination, future job interviews must include information about your past employment. What you share should be as complete and truthful and as positive as possible. The more recent your termination, the more significant it will be as a factor in the overall hiring process. If your interviewer asks for more information, impart what you learned from the termination and how you believe the termination has made you a better prospective employee than you might have otherwise been. Be absolutely truthful about the circumstances, and avoid playing the "victim card", even if you believe it applies.

If you are the interviewer, seek as much information as you believe you need in order to make your decision regarding the applicant. Do not over estimate or under estimate the importance of the prior termination. What did the interviewee take from the experience and why might he or she enjoy success in the job for which he or she is applying?

Reason 2: Downsizing

In the Introduction, we discussed companies' efforts to do more with less, especially when it comes to total employment. Rare is the production process today that involves human capital cost that exceeds about 20 percent of total costs, yet attempts to downsize by reducing employment seem to be continuous and not confined to production processes only. Virtually every change that is completed has as a component of consideration the effect of implementation of employment reductions. In today's corporate environment, the possibility of being personally impacted by downsizing is more real than ever. We could go on and on with a discussion of the reasons for downsizing and whether they are legitimate or effective, but when you are faced with the reality, the reasons don't really matter.

Our chapter on mergers, acquisitions and joint ventures also alludes to the potential for downsizing as a means to cut costs, streamline operations and eliminate positions that are now duplicated or otherwise unnecessary. Management positions at all levels are at risk in a post-merger environment as individuals and departments jockey for positions.

What may separate the act of downsizing from termination is your company's response to dealing with each type of event. As opposed to termination, downsizing may be accompanied by severance pay, some continuation of fringe benefits such as health care for a period of time, and job placement assistance. Certainly this assistance helps to soften the blow, but the fact remains that downsizing means the end to employment—maybe in a job and with a company that you love and where your performance has been above reproach. Negotiate the best deal you can, and take advantage of any benefits and assistance that the company has to offer.

The fact that downsizing may be done with some reluctance by the company and concern for the morale of those who remain does not make it any less inevitable if your position is targeted for elimination.

Move on with as much dignity and understanding as you can muster. Try not to take it personally. More times than you know, corporate employment reductions (i.e., downsizing) are part of a scattergun approach to accomplishing a cost-cutting goal that may or may not be achievable, and may not be good for business long term if the cost cuts are achieved.

Your subsequent interviews should be thoughtful, not vindictive and not cast in such a was as to make you a victim, even though you likely are. Find a positive way to present the situation and let your overall attitude be positive and motivated about your future at XYZ Company.

Reason 3: Resignation

Virtually all employees find themselves in this position at least once in their working life. While much more desirable than termination, it is often no less stressful. Employees resign primarily for one of three reasons: (1) They have discovered a different job or a sought-after opportunity has presented itself, (2) they are ready for retirement, or (3) they are disillusioned with the current situation.

In the last instance, once triggered, their disillusionment feeds on every situation that may arise, focusing on the negative factors that accompany almost every action, if one looks hard enough. They have been passed over for a promotion or a desirable assignment. They have been passed over for a mentoring program. Their job duties are not as advertised and they hate their job. They are convinced that advancement potential does not exist in the reasonable future. They have convinced themselves that management doesn't have a clue and the very survival of the company is in doubt.

All valid reasons for moving on, but with the exception of the instance of hating your job, all of the above are perceptions that may or may not reflect reality. All the same, moving on is usually for the best. Choose carefully what disillusionments you will share at the exit interview. Your final act could be the gift of truthful, helpful information to your former employer that will help the company in its future plans, which no doubt includes choosing your replacement.

At post resignation interviews, share what information you believe is appropriate, but keep details to a truthful minimum. Sharing your disillusionment and despair over aspects of your prior job will only serve to create a sense of doubt in the mind of your prospective employer. Be focused in the future, with a positive outlook and attitude.

Job interviews following any of the situations we have discussed can be awkward and stressful. Practice interviewing skills with a friend or co-worker to prepare yourself for any eventualities. Asking and answering the tough questions at this point will make the real thing a lot loss stressful. Give and get honest, constructive feedback that will be helpful in future interview situations.

Rarely is termination, downsizing or resignation the end of the road. To a large extent it is what you make of it, so make the most of it.

CONCLUSION

"I firmly believe that any man's finest hour—the greatest
fulfillment to all he holds dear—is the moment when he
has worked his heart out in a good cause and lies
exhausted on the field of battle—victorious."
—Vincent Lombardi

When I was in school, we studied a period of time in history known as the industrial revolution. In case you have forgotten (or never knew), the industrial revolution was a period of time beginning in the late 18th century and continuing until the early years of the 20th century, that we can identify, looking back, as a period of tremendous technological advancement and cultural and socioeconomic change.

This period of time was, of course, not known as the industrial revolution to those who were citizens of the time. To them it was simply a period in history when the technology that existed and was exploited by the creative genius of the times resulted in new inventions that offered the tools to make their lives easier or more productive. They embraced and exploited that technology, which in turn created the need for additional tools, which continued the revolution.

The term "revolution" is not too strong a descriptive term to be used to characterize this period. Most of the technology that was developed, beginning primarily in Britain and America, and spreading east through Europe, would be considered rudimentary when compared with today's almost-sentient machinery. Nevertheless, the innovations, however basic, were so significant in meeting the needs for increased productivity that change came rapidly and of necessity. Nothing that could have been planned or anticipated could have prepared people for what was occurring all around them. With, we imagine, some sense of wonderment at the pace of innovation, people generally were only too eager to make the necessary adjustments to accommodate innovation.

The cultural and socioeconomic shifts that accompanied and were in many cases necessitated by the technology were tremendous and shaped the way we live and work today. In retrospect, we begin to understand the monumental changes that occurred and to admire society's ability to assimilate the new technology and respond to the changes it brought to bear on individuals and groups in our culture.

For the first time, a majority of men left to work outside the homestead during the workweek and were no longer as available to their children. America began its shift away from an agrarian society to one based upon processing, manufacturing, and distribution of goods. Development and innovations in each of these areas was necessitated by, and often accomplished by, the growth in manufacturing-based innovation.

This was also a period of tremendous global upheaval. Not a subject of this book, suffice it to say that innovation continued sometimes in spite of, not because of, new international alliances and growing political friction. Innovation was an unstoppable force. Think of the innovation potential from just one change—the switch from steam power to electric power.

All of this was accompanied by great personal change. Literacy skyrocketed, fueled by innovation and improvements in the printing industry, which made printed materials available to the common man, both in terms of availability and price. Communication improved in terms of both the accuracy and the speed of the message. What a tremendous period in which to live.

Not all was uplifting, however. Crime was rampant as law enforcement failed to keep pace with burgeoning populations in new cities. Medical and dental care and public sanitation were less than desirable. The industrial revolution did not solve all problems simultaneously. It was not until late in the period that necessities such as running potable water, electricity, and refrigeration became commonly available. Maybe the good old days weren't.

Socioeconomic change was also evident as a new class of capitalists began to form. Henry Ford and others who mastered the practical application of new industrial machinery made financial fortunes, and the "industrialists" joined and eventually largely replaced the landowners and the lumber barons as the rich and powerful among us.

About 150 years later, we are in the midst of a "technological revolution" that is no less significant in terms of its effect on individuals, families, and society. For some perspective, talk to a 70-, 80-, or 90-year-old senior citizen about what it was like "back in the day" and learn what socioeconomic and cultural changes have been adopted by our society in response to technological advances. History must, to be accurate, record this current time as a period of unparalleled growth in innovation and information.

People today wonder why there are no more people like Thomas Edison inventing technological marvels that will revolutionize our life. The fact is that there are "Thomas Edisons" throughout our society and the world, bringing us technological advances almost daily that would be awe-inspiring were we not in such a mad rush to employ and exploit this technology to benefit and advance our lives. In our "what have you done for me lately" society, we spend little or no time thinking about what it takes to bring the Next Big Thing to market and what special people they are who are responsible for making our achievements a reality.

It seems sometimes that we have almost overnight assimilation of totally new or revolutionary products into our society. For example, the cell phone almost overnight made the then-ubiquitous pager obsolete and quickly went on to become a virtual necessity, changing our lives in fundamental ways that we may possibly only appreciate from a historical perspective. There are hundreds of examples of products that we simply begin to use and immediately depend upon, as if they had always been available.

When I purchased my first "pocket calculator" (for about $45), I could purchase with it optional extended warranty protection. Today, calculators are powered by (amazing) photovoltaic components or are virtually disposable because the price of a new (another amazing product) battery equals the price of a new calculator.

Today, we admire and recognize the efforts and achievements of Thomas Edison, Alexander Graham Bell, Orville and Wilbur Wright, Eli Whitney, and so many others whose inventiveness so enriched our lives. Will our children and our grandchildren recognize the names William Shockley, Walter Brattain, and John Bardeen as the Nobel Prize-winning inventors of the transistor—arguably the greatest invention of the 20th century? It is likely that they will not. Why? Because we recognize most that which we understand and which most directly touches our lives. So it is that Messrs. Shockley, Brattain, and Bardeen will remain in obscurity, as will others who added capacitors, resistors, and memory to the transistor to bring us the "chip" we all know and use every day.

Who gets the credit in terms of public recognition and appreciation? Steve Jobs and Steven Wozniak employed the chip in the first "home computer" from Apple. They earned our respect and admiration (and a great deal of money) by exploiting a breakthrough product (i.e., a new invention—the computer chip) that was largely ignored by the public until its usefulness became apparent.

Recognition comes when invention and application merge for the good of all, resulting in timely useful innovations.

There is a cognitive component to the technological revolution. It is that as technology is advancing, at an exponential pace, we understand less and less about the "how" and "why" as it relates to the workings of the technology on which we have become totally dependent. This is a bit unsettling to those of us who like to understand why things are what they are and why they do what they do. Others have no interest in such matters, which does not seem to affect their employment and enjoyment of new equipment.

Does the evolutionary process of the battery, from alkaline to ni-cad to lithium-ion, matter to the average consumer? Probably not. Are the technical advantages promised by quantum computing appreciated and understood by those who will soon be utilizing its amazing capabilities? Probably not. I will confess that I do not understand most of what I read about quantum computing, but that will not prevent me from availing myself of its power in my daily pursuits when it becomes available. As one who used to tinker with confidence under the hood of his 1957 Chevy, I can attest to the changes in motor vehicle technology. (As the word *advancement* is not universally applicable here, I have instead chosen to use the word *changes*—the reader can draw his or her own conclusions.)

As one looks forward, it would be hard for the human mind to overestimate the technological, cultural, and socioeconomic changes yet to come. What technology lies ahead? What problems are we solving? What problems are we creating? Nationally and globally, how will we accommodate individuals who are not necessary in the product-providing and service-providing economies of the world? Are there moral and ethical components to innovations that must be debated and resolved? Will government intervention derail innovation? Is unchecked, unregulated innovation always good? Is global warming a threat? If so, can its effects be mitigated by human intervention? Will technology serve to make us more independent, one from another?

So many questions, so many changes. If you look, change is all around us. For example, do you travel to a trade show to look at a new product or simply pull up an online video? Has the Internet and teleconferencing made business travel obsolete? Is it productive to show up at the airport three hours early for a two-hour flight to attend a four-hour meeting? How we respond to change in one area of our lives can have a dynamic effect on other areas, as our teleconferencing/travel example illustrates.

Most of the questions I posed above will not be answered by our technology; we will answer them as individuals and as a collective society. I don't have the answers; I don't even know all the questions. I do know that we cannot abdicate the management of the direction of our society and our cultural heritage to technology-based decisions. Individuals will need all the attributes discussed in this book in abundance far into the future, both independently and corporately. Technology will make some jobs obsolete but will cause the evolution of new frontiers and will expose areas that need to be addressed by individuals and governments in order to maintain a civilized society.

Today, we are rushing to employ each and every new technological innovation that appears, with the promise that our lives will be made easier or fuller or more productive thereby. At the same time, we read in our business publications that people are working longer days and longer weeks, are taking their laptops and BlackBerries on working vacations, and are under more stress than ever before. What do we make of this perceived dichotomy? I believe these lifestyle changes manifest some of the cultural and socioeconomic shifts that are taking place today in response to new technology.

Like a drug, a new tech toy or tech tool can be used or abused. We fret about adolescent preoccupation with video gaming, but what about Mr. or Mrs. Businessperson sitting by the pool with the laptop fired up while the rest of the family enjoys its vacation, or a cell phone glued to his or her ear while others enjoy dinner at a restaurant (the pet peeve of many), or thumbing the BlackBerry far into the night? To be unconnected is to be out of touch. Something might happen, we think, and our response or input is too vital to be omitted. We would do well to take a collective step back and ask ourselves where we are headed as individuals and as a society. Have we become slaves to the very technology that can make life "better"? Some would say yes and have no problem with that. Others would say we've gone too far but there's no turning back. We have many restaurants today going "smokeless." Can the "phoneless" restaurant be far behind? Is it really such a bad idea?

What do you say? How will history be recorded this time? Will historians use some technological descendent of the computer or a quill pen to record it? We are not in control of how future historians record this period in time, but we can control much of how we live our life today. That's one action plan that we really need to work on.

AN INVITATION

Do you have an interesting or unusual story about life in the corporate environment? Have you employed an unusual or innovative management practice in order to achieve a desired result? Why was it or wasn't it successful? Is your company's management style especially successful in achieving a specific corporate goal or mission? Does your company employ unusual or innovative motivational techniques? Has your company implemented changes that backfired or resulted in unintended (good or bad) consequences? Is an unusual management style undeniably successful at your place of work? Does your company continue traditional methods of operation to the company's detriment or benefit? Has your company discovered unique and profitable methods of dealing with its competitors?

If you would like to share any of these or other related examples or instances with others, we would like to hear from you. Our next book is intended to be a compilation of stories about managers' successes, failures, and innovative responses to situations and circumstances that occur in corporate life. Your name and your company's name will not be used. All submissions are confidential, and those furnishing an example that is used will receive a free copy of the book. You can play a part in helping others make better management decisions! Send us your e-mail at *thenext-book@usa.net*—and thanks for your participation!